THE TRADING BOOK

THE TRADING BOOK

A COMPLETE SOLUTION TO MASTERING
TECHNICAL SYSTEMS AND TRADING PSYCHOLOGY

ANNE-MARIE BAIYND

New York Chicago San Francisco Lisbon London Madrid Mexico City
Milan New Delhi San Juan Seoul Singapore Sydney Toronto

1 2 3 4 5 6 7 8 9 10 11 12 13 14 15   QFR/QFR   1 9 8 7 6 5 4 3 2 1

ISBN 978-0-07-176649-4
MHID   0-07-176649-9

e-ISBN 978-0-07-176700-2
e-MHID   0-07-176700-2

This publication is designed to provide accurate and authoritative information in regard to the subject matter covered. It is sold with the understanding that neither the author nor the publisher is engaged in rendering legal, accounting, securities trading, or other professional services. If legal advice or other expert assistance is required, the services of a competent professional person should be sought.
> —*From a Declaration of Principles Jointly Adopted by a Committee of the American Bar Association and a Committee of Publishers and Associations*

Charts courtesy of Tony Lindsay, MotiveWave Software

McGraw-Hill books are available at special quantity discounts to use as premiums and sales promotions or for use in corporate training programs. To contact a representative, please e-mail us at bulksales@mcgraw-hill.com.

This book is printed on acid-free paper.

*Dedicated to the most warm, wonderful, and supportive man in
all the world, my husband, Tony, who stood beside me
in the deepest valleys, steadfast and true, always believing in me
so much more than I ever believed in myself*

*Dedicated to the most warm, wonderful, and supportive man in
all the world, my husband, Tony, who stood beside me
in the deepest valleys, steadfast and true, always believing in me
so much more than I ever believed in myself*

Contents

Acknowledgments   ix

Introduction   xiii

CHAPTER 1   **An Introduction to the Markets**   1

CHAPTER 2   **Technical Indicators I**
MARKET POSITIONING SYSTEM, MOMENTUM,
AND CANDLESTICKS   **15**

CHAPTER 3   **Technical Indicators II**
MOVING AVERAGES, BOLLINGER BANDS,
AND VOLUME   **29**

CHAPTER 4   **Trading Well Is Not Only About
Trading Systems**   **47**

CHAPTER 5   **Trading Blind and Risk**   **59**

CHAPTER 6   **Waves and Fibonaccis**   **75**

CHAPTER 7   **You Deserve Success**   93

CHAPTER 8   **From Simple to Complex: Long Trade**   103

CHAPTER 9   **Your Trading Journal**   135

CHAPTER 10   **From Simple to Complex: Short Trade**   149

CHAPTER 11   **Discipline, Dedication, and Endurance**   181

CHAPTER 12   **The Ideal Trade Setup**   193

CHAPTER 13   **Nuances of Chart Formations**   207

CHAPTER 14   **A Recap of the Technical and
Temperamental Skill Sets**   223

CHAPTER 15   **Self-Preservation and Support Structures**   233

Conclusion   241

Glossary   245

Index   251

Acknowledgments

"Gratitude is not only the greatest of virtues, but the parent of all the others."

—MARCUS TULLIUS CICERO

I've been so fortunate to meet the wonderful people I have in the business of trading, but there have been a few folks whom I would be most remiss if I did not let know what a solid support structure they have been to me. Though I did dedicate this book to my husband, I have to say once again that without his encouragement and belief in my abilities, I would have never made it. He was my backbone when I thought the market had broken it. It has made the triumph so much sweeter. Thank you, my sweetheart—I have been blessed beyond words by the life I live with you.

To Brian Shannon, of AlphaTrends.net, I say a very special thank-you—you taught me the "art of calm," to look for the beauty of the general simplicity of the market. Your book, *Technical Analysis Using Multiple Timeframes*, is one of the best technical studies I have ever read, and your tools at http://www.alphascanner.com provide superb stock picks to trade consistently. You sent me on the search for structure, form, and pattern development sitting clearly in the market, and you were generous with your time, your vast technical knowledge, your energy, and your recommendations. Never have I met anyone in the work world who is so willing to share knowledge and insight with aspiring traders; I owe a great deal of where I am today to you, and for that I am so very, very grateful.

A special thanks goes to Kathy G., largely responsible for the Glossary at the end of the book, a huge supporter and a cornerstone to TheTradingBook.com, a loyal friend, a tireless worker, a true craftsman and perpetual student in the trading world, and to Dennis M., Apple fanatic, staunch supporter, and a linchpin to holding the room together with Kathy over the years. You both have been wonderful teachers and educators in your own right at TheTrading Book.com, and I could not do it nearly as well without you.

Thank you, also, to the hardest-working and most conscientious students I have had in all my years of coaching. Each of you kept me working harder knowing that we were all growing together in trading strength, and you did just as much to lift my spirits and skills as I did yours, without a doubt—Brenda C., Mike T., Kim P., Dean J., Tariq M., Stanton K., and Neil W., the most naturally talented trader I have ever had the good fortune of coaching.

To my room of wonderful longtime contributing traders at TheTradingBook.com, who have supported me, silently and openly, held my feet to the fire, and without whom I could not have developed the honed skills I have today, Steve D., Blaine, Milan, Ben, Jack, Maddie, Mike E., Karl, Tom B., Dick S., Gary, Lina, Liz, Pete, and Paul, thanks. We make for a powerhouse of traders; we really do.

More thank-yous and notes of gratitude go to John Lee of Charts GoneWild.com and CEO of Lee Capital Management—champion, defender, and welcome room-disrupter; Howard Lindzon and Phil Pearlman for allowing me to be part of the StockTwits network; the wonderful team of trading leaders and helpful staff in the trading space at StockTwits.com; MotiveWave.com for an incredible charting software that gave these illustrations life; Damien Hoffman and WallStCheatSheet.com for their open sponsorship and support; Fari Hamzei, Kevin Hughes, and Mike Bellafiore, for being great exchangers of knowledge and trading insight; and Stephanie Frerich and McGraw-Hill for providing an accommodating and encouraging work environment that made writing this piece of work a joy.

Last but most important, I want to thank my Lord and Savior, Jesus Christ, for helping me through this journey. He kept me grounded, helped me keep balance in my life, and led me to wise study, wise people, and wise behavior. His still small voice kept me going in my most isolated moments. Every single solitary piece of success I have ever had, and ever will have, I owe to my Lord, and I live a life of joy unspeakable: content, comforted, and fulfilled to know that I do not run under my own steam but under the infinite power of the universe that comes from God.

Introduction

"Just tell me where to buy and sell." As both an educator and market moderator, I have discovered this is the most common mindset of the novice retail trader entering the market, lured by the promise of 1,000% returns. The truth is that trading is a tough business, and if it were as easy as the use of a cookie-cutter approach to buy and sell and make 1,000% returns, the distribution of wealth in the market would be much more evenly spread. Instead, it is bottom-heavy, and top-light.

When entering the trading world, most of what we knew about the market was cursory, but we did well enough in our past professional pursuits to believe that what made us successful previously would somehow translate into successful trading in our future. It certainly was a big surprise to me to learn that trading every day in the market is a unique career requiring special skills executed in a manner quite contrary to the way our minds actually function ordinarily. It is usually only after many market losses that we are able to discover that our playing field is a beast all its own, the players all in a very specific game with precise rules of engagement, and the average retail trader, as I was, running in the field, extraordinarily and completely oblivious to many of the rules.

The retail trader is like that great kid from Pop Warner League, full of promise and burgeoning skill, stepping on the gridiron, only our opponents are the Pittsburgh Steelers—one of us, all of them.

Get the picture? That, folks, is the reality for most individual retail traders, and it is why most retail traders, well, really suck. We don't know what we don't know! Then, by the time we discover and figure out what it was we didn't know in the first place, the market has a brand new twist for us. For many of us, it takes a lot of losses to learn what we didn't know—if we ever do so at all. Frankly, most traders don't learn what is necessary and run out of money before they ever fully understand the rules of the game.

I am an unusual professional trader as I am completely self-taught, without influence or exposure to the "Wall Street" crowd particularly. Warren Buffett, who has spent his life and career thousands of miles away from New York in Omaha, Nebraska, has said often that one of the best things he has ever done is stay far away from the people on "the Street." Though I can only speculate what he might have truly meant by that, I know that philosophy holds true for me.

Realizing I am easily influenced by other market opinions, I took a sequestered approach to study, and although I chose a few people to learn from, particularly Brian Shannon of AlphaTrends .net, I decided to carve out my own system built on simplicity and raw observable data. People's opinions affect us much more than we might think they do, and since most people do very poorly in the market, well, you can finish the sentence.

The deliberate avoidance of the "expert opinions" allowed me to develop a clean, clear technical trading system from my own personal observations over years of study and application that continues to perform well daily. As I continued to trade and tweet in real time on my trades (on Twitter, @annemarietrades), I began to hear from many traders asking about ideas and positions. From the line of questioning, it became apparent to me that most people trading are adrift with a poorly developed set of skills, preventing them from developing excellence independently. Most retail traders follow trades somewhat blindly, have completely unrealistic expectations, and end up with hit-and-miss performance (mostly miss) because the rationale needed to trade well is clearly absent. In the mean-

time, traders consistently race across the minefield of psychological pitfalls that accompany a lack of confidence, internal knowledge, trading competence, and market understanding while experiencing fears of loss and failure. Desperate for gains, they chase screaming or apparently accelerating stocks or follow other traders, resulting in a cauldron of doomed trades. They are really just gambling with their holdings, desperately wanting to be, and do, more. They hope to trade well and succeed but lack a compass to deliver true direction. This evidence of a clear absence of trading aptitude, skill, and psychological mindset in the average trader in the stream moved me to write this book.

The market is a war with some savvy people who would like nothing more than to relieve us of our account holdings. There is a game taking place 24 hours a day, 7 days a week, in any given market. There is no "free hand of economics" alive in the market; every day, stocks, futures, bonds, and options are all manipulated by the able and the crafty, and if we aren't nervous about that with our investing, we should be. If we are entering the market with a lack of skill, we're asking to be roadkill. This book will reveal this playing field, and how, as an individual retail trader, we can triumph over our competition so that we might join the ranks of the competent, confident, and successful trader.

Join me on the step-by-step journey to discover a pure, simple trading system, and learn to implement it through direct, real-life trading events so that you, too, can say proudly, "Yes, I am a good professional trader," and have the results to show for it.

CHAPTER 1

An Introduction to the Markets

"You cannot step twice into the same rivers; for other waters are ever flowing onto you."

—HERACLITUS

As long as we keep conscious of the fact that the markets are a living enterprise, run by fickle, changeable beings, we'll grip the notion that they are never the same place twice. As Mark Twain once said, "History does not repeat itself, it merely rhymes." The same is true of markets. The general "introduction to the markets" chapter normally describes the basic structure of the markets with equities, futures, forex, or some other trading instrument. Although that is important, and the structures are a good thing to understand, I will leave that to other authors. The nature of this work suggests we take an alternate view of the market at the outset in the not-so-typical way—not the overview of the forest, but a look through the trees while keeping very aware of the fact that we are in a forest.

This view is even more unusual when we consider that our approach to trading will be largely technical in nature. Our ability to grasp this view, however, will assist us in observing the market as an entity, not just an amalgam of technical pieces, and that, in turn, will transform you into a trader who thinks on a grand and, at the same time, granular scale.

By accepting that the market is an entity in constant flux, we cannot approach trading in a cookie-cutter manner, no matter how much we would like to. Instead, to trade at maximum efficiency, we must set that cookie cutter aside to make real tracks toward our end goal of superior, consistent returns. The same actions will not always be required in response to occurrences of the same type all the time. Did the full impact of that sentence seep through? The markets are never exactly in the same place twice, and each time we witness a technical event, the meaning of that event may not be the same as the last time we saw it. The markets require that we remain in a thinking and analytic state in order to perform well within it.

Here's what I mean: if the general rule is "short below the moving average break or crossover," that might not be the specific action you need to implement due to another extraneous event also unfolding. The day is never as simple as the "if-then" statement. If you are looking for that kind of road map in trading, your search will be exhausting, never ending, and oh, by the way, an exercise in futility. It is never as simple as "tell me when to buy and sell." Trading well means we are always discerning and appraising. We will need the power of discretionary thought to move through our trades. Only then will we achieve excellence in performance. This notion unnerves many newer traders because we all realize that there are things we don't know. The problem is that we just don't know that we don't know these things until we realize we didn't know them in the first place, and that comes only after we know them, no? By then, the market has usually charged us dearly for the access to the knowledge. Right? Yes, the road most traveled, indeed. So how do we navigate the markets as a technician? In order to answer that question, we must ask ourselves the following question.

WHAT IS TECHNICAL TRADING?

Technical trading uses charting methods and analyses to determine market movement. Completely different to fundamental analysis, all technical analysis uses are the formations that the charts develop as the stocks move through particular price points. It is a method that assumes there is a way to discover patterns that accurately predict future events based on prior market formations. Technical trading attempts to identify areas of entry and exit that skew our chances of being correct to greater than a coin toss (fifty-fifty). The use of technical indicators does not imply causality; that is, one event does not cause the other. Instead, we approach the technicals in the framework that they have a likelihood of appearing together. This can also be called *probability bias*.

In case the following thought has not occurred prior to this moment, we actually use probability bias in every aspect of our lives. Some of the most common events utilize the bias, such as knowing that if you see the mailman driving down the street, it is likely that your mailbox will have something in it shortly. Will it happen every single time? Maybe not, but it sure does happen a lot. Does our mailman cause us to have mail? No, he does not. What causes us to have mail is the person or persons who mailed us. He just happened to be the conduit of transport. What about the caller ID on our phone showing the chattiest friend we have calling? We are quite aware that if we answer it, it is most likely that we'll be on the phone for a while. Will our friend talk ad nauseam every time? Perhaps, and perhaps not. Again, it is the possibility of the event that we are considering that causes us to contemplate a decision. So it is with technical trading.

We work on identifying patterns that seem to happen in clusters, and we choose to make decisions based on what we assume is highly probable of occurring. We make the choices simple, but decisions to execute and act will always be less than completely straightforward. Our ability to discern the minor shifts in the market action that might require us to take the extra step, waiting for further confirmation (another signal) before our decision to enter or exit the trade, will be the delineator between success and failure.

REALITY AND PERCEPTION

Many of us think of the market as a logical mechanism. People who are not acutely aware of markets and how they operate will argue this fact without ceasing. In fact, there are scores of intellectual economic studies that try to reassure us that Adam Smith's notion of the free hand of the market (the natural order and market laws of supply and demand will drive market efficiencies to maximum output and fairness) operates well, and hence it is sufficient for markets to function without intervention. There are also scores of other books that suggest that Keynesian economics (a theory that states that government intervention is not only favorable but highly necessary for markets to run well) is necessary for order in markets to continue.

Markets aren't really orderly though, and they are never in balance for more than an instant—if ever. The market is a giant pendulum that swings from one extreme to the other, forced there by a variety of reasons that numerous pundits pontificate (inaccurately many times) daily. If we know the market operates as a giant swing, then as traders we must work at being keenly aware of the direction of the oscillations and signals that accompany tipping points, which often lead to reversal. There are no markets that operate efficiently on a consistent basis; instead, the ebb and flow caused by sentiment shift, panic, euphoria, greed, and disbelief drives us through the peaks and valleys. If we can firmly cement this simple concept, we will avoid one of the worst mistakes an inexperienced trader will make: trading what we think and not what we see.

Sometimes It Is Best Not to Trade What You Think

Sounds like an oxymoron, doesn't it? Yes, this statement does need some qualifiers, so here they are. First, if we think something seems logical, we need to wait for the market to prove us out before we go "all in on margin" because we are sure of what the market will do next. Second, simply because something makes sense doesn't mean the market will respond in the way we think it will or at the time we think it will. Here's an example: Every Thursday, initial jobless claims are reported at 8:30 A.M. Let's say we've been watching the news, and we've seen long lines at the unemployment office on television, or we've been talking to people all over who reveal the same information: the job market is soft. So we know that the number is going to be bad, and when the number is bad, the market usually takes a dip.

So the night before, stepping in front of the trade, we decide we are going to take a short position to capitalize on the market dip— we load up on the SDS, or go short SPY, or short ES_F (the e-mini futures), or simply go long the SPX puts before the close of the day. We are very keen and excited about trading this piece of news giving us the "edge" and the jump on catching the dip.

Thursday morning, as we suspect, the numbers are dreadful, but amazingly, the market moves upward (does this story sound familiar to anyone?). Why? We were correct in our anticipation of the poor numbers release. Did we look to see what the projected number was going to be? Did we notice if the market was pulling back days before and thus pricing the number in? These are market nuances that the new retail trader spends little time reviewing and, because of it, she ends up on the wrong side of the trade. One of many news flashes: trading the news can be hit or miss, and, mostly, it is miss.

So why is it that we don't need to trade what seems logical? Because we are not privy to all the moving parts often, and making decisions with a lack of proper information leads to poor choices in the trading realm. Now, as we develop skill, market knowledge, and understanding of basic market rhythms, what seems logical will come closer to what we expect, but no matter how much we think we understand, it is always the best discretion to let the market show us where it is going and just simply follow (this would be prudent), rather than predict where the market is going and place a position (this would be gambling).

Markets Are Not for Gambling

As I try to introduce people to the mechanics of technical trading, I am often hit with the statement "you're just gambling," or "it's just gambling, trading in the market." Many people think of and approach the market as a large casino. We come in with five thousand and expect to leave with a million at the end of the month. OK, I'm exaggerating—we expect to leave with, say, ten thousand. (Realize that we expose ourselves to this same "gambling" element if we opt to participate in a 401(k), or anything that uses our liquid capital to multiply itself.)

In my experience, many traders from the retail side who come into trading fall into it—they lose their primary source of income and decide that they will trade their 401(k) to generate copious amounts of cash and quickly move to basking in the Tahitian sunshine. Or they enter with a small account, lured by the promise of extraordinary success (usually through outrageous advertising), and trade with completely unrealistic expectations and, by default, an extremely high level of risk.

It is highly likely that if we entered the market as an average retail trader, our hopes were most likely unrealistic due to a large gap in our knowledge of how and when markets move, and why. Also possible is that we don't understand just how much risk it takes to magnify our accounts to such extremes. So many traders come in expecting to make 10, 20, 50 times the returns of the greatest investors and traders of our time. Why is that? A lack of knowledge, understanding, and perspective.

Markets Take Years to Master

I'd like you to ask yourself, "What do I expect out of my performance?" I had a very inexperienced person ask me, "I have a $20K account, and I would like to replace my current income of $120,000 a year. Can you help me do that?" Let's look at that question phrased another way: "I am a novice trader with little technical skill. I have an account limited by day-trading rules that allow me only three day trades in every five trading days, and with that, I would like to generate $10K a month consistently all year—that's 50% returns a month, or 600% a year." Yeah, sure, that sounds reasonable—*not*!

Here's another one: "I was hoping you could teach me everything you know. I have a $2K account, and I would like to generate 1% a day. Is that feasible?" Well, if you think about the fact that there are approximately 260 trading days in a year, you're asking for 260% return, *and* you are unskilled and trading a very small account. Is that even a rational thought?

I'm not here to quash personal aspirations, but we all need to be reasonable in our expectations and begin to think like professionals, not amateurs. In order for us to be successful, we must come to terms with what we have at our disposal, realize our limitations, build on our weaknesses, and position ourselves to be winners. Returns of 200%–600% each year are possible, but not probable, for the average, and even above-average, trader. Returns like that carry enormous amounts of risk and usually take accounts to ruin. Some of the greatest traders and investors of our time lost sight of risk, began to gamble, and ended up destroyed and penniless. If we can agree that gains like the ones just mentioned are less than common, what can we expect from a perspective of practicality working in the market? That answer solely depends on what it is we know and how well we are able to use what we know.

WHAT DO WE ACTUALLY KNOW ABOUT THE MARKET?

What we know about the market is impossibly difficult to identify if we are novice traders. There are two types of information in the market:

1. Actionable information
2. Everything else

Certainly, I write that a bit tongue in cheek, but becoming successful is not about amassing vast quantities of information based on economic theory and general market relationships. There are a lot of brilliant, highly informed, and intelligent people in the financial space who have no trading ability whatsoever. Lots of knowledge or understanding of what are thought to be general market dynamics does not necessarily make for a good trader. Only the application of very specific knowledge at a very specific time will make for good trades. Everything else is noise.

The Importance of Filtering Noise

We filter noise every moment of our waking lives. We filter overhead music and the din of the crowd to hear our dinner guests' chatter. We lose focus of the music in our car so that we can pick up the sound of the fire engine closing ground behind us. We filter our senses by lack of attention to the sensory input. This is a necessary element of our existence, and in fact, our ability to thrive as human beings. When it comes to trading, however, we forget how important this mechanism is to our survival. We lose our ability to filter the necessary from the unnecessary. Maybe because we believe more is always better, we choose to go after as much information as possible. I am not saying this is incorrect. What I am saying is that if your answer to the question "Why am I collecting this information?" is " So that I can trade better," and you still do not trade more successfully with the accumulation of information, there is a problem to be addressed.

Filtering garbage from usable data will be one of the most difficult things we will ever have to do as a short-term swing or day trader. What does this garbage look like? Simply, it is wrapped in a package of opinion, not based purely on verifiable data; it is conjecture without evidence. If we can avoid most of this, our trading will become less clouded by what the latest "smartest guy in the room" says. Problem is, most of the things we hear on television and the radio, and much of what we read, is pure conjecture. Here's a fact: just because someone is on television and being touted doesn't make him or her right.

I have a tendency to focus a lot on the importance of focus. Focus is everything and will make or break your trading day. I've heard from several senior partners at different trading firms that they do not allow their traders to watch any news television during their trading day solely so they stay concentrated on their task at hand. With every student I have ever coached, they all begin with a lack of focus on the charts and too much focus on what they are reading, or hearing, or watching outside of the charts. Charts will tell you the outcome of any truth before any average person will. Granted, there are those few in the market who seem to have outstanding fundamentals calls. They get in front of the trade and are right, but even they are looking at charts, though not the ones we, day traders, concentrate on.

It is best to view our charts as canvases, because they all do paint a picture. Granted some look like M. C. Escher or Picasso paintings (you know you're looking at something, but you're not *quite* sure what it is), but many others are simple connect-the-dots types. We just have to work on seeing which dots to connect. The decisions we make on choosing which dots to connect make trading part art and part science. When we work with charts, almost every one of us needs to look just a little closer and think a little harder as we view them. Trading is a thinking person's game, and if we do not have the ability to reason through what we might see within the charts, we will consistently have difficulty in the field.

So how might we filter noise? Reading the news is fine: I am not advocating that you stop reading your favorite news blogs or opinion editorials. I only ask you to remember that people throw in what they think all the time in the midst of these facts. Everyone writing or speaking has an angle they want to deliver—if you view the world like that, making decisions with information presented to you will be much more simple. It is imperative to cultivate discernment between skew and raw data.

Try not to listen to pundits during the day. Pay attention to *facts*, not what people think. If someone says something you would like to pay attention to and apply to your trading, look for the facts to corroborate the ideas this person has brought up, and try to understand the time frame for which he or she presents the argument. Traders spend a lot of time taking trades based on what people think only to discover later that the comment was made with respect to a five-year time line, not a two-week one.

The market is considered a forward pricing mechanism for companies, so it is likely that by the time the release is out to the public, much of the insider market has already priced this in. The rule of thumb is this: the more you jump in front of a trade because of what you perceive as market-moving news, the more likely your account balance will fluctuate. Of course, this is not always the case—but I do want to caution you against this kind of gunslinger mentality.

The Importance of Timing

There is also the irksome notion of timing. If someone with a great track record says he is bullish on the market, how do we actually know about the time frame he is discussing? Does he mean the next year, the next month, the next week, or the next day? Many of us make decisions on what we hear from what others say without any thought of the length of time that is associated with the trade. That is a breeding ground for calamity. We may as well aim the gun for our foot. Here's what I mean.

In Figure 1.1, consider that you and I are on the opposite sides of a trade. You are long and I am short. If I make my trade entry at point X and exit at point Y, my trade is considered a success. If you make a trade entry at point A and exit at point B, your trade is considered a success. Same day, same chart—different trades, both successes.

The point is this: if we hear someone say she is short or long something—doesn't it stand to reason that we take the time to discover the time frames in consideration? Yet, as an ill-equipped trader, time frames often do not enter our sphere of consciousness when making trading decisions. We'll be discussing time frames briefly as they relate to trading perspective in Chapter 12, but be

Figure 1.1 **Candlestick Chart**

aware that appropriate time-frame decisions can be the reason for both success and failure.

In short, pay attention to formations as opposed to general market banter that is no more useful than arguing with our friends about which sports team is best. The chart configurations will always reveal trend and tend to telegraph directional trajectory repetitively.

Markets Are Manipulated; You Can Trade Them Anyway

I read disgruntled traders' comments in the Twitter stream all the time complaining about manipulated markets. Some may say this is paranoia, but those of us close to the pits or privy to behind-the-scenes machinations of the giant brokerage houses know that this is a plain and simple truth. Here's some advice: roll with it, and stop complaining about something out of your control. Listen, even if this manipulation is real, the market is capable of being traded in an organized manner, and as long as we remain comfortable that the market rhythm can be tracked, estimated, predicted, and replicated by our system, we'll be fine.

I have a trading colleague—let's call him Mr. X (that ought to be vague enough for anyone wondering if I am describing him). Mr. X is an experienced market maker who has seen the market shift from an organized cause-and-effect environment to one he clearly believes is manipulated daily by machines. For months we would work together, and I would say at the beginning of every day, "Hey, we are going to trade what we see." And every day, without fail, he would trade what he *thought*, because what he thought had made him money prior. The process of reengineering our minds is problematic for us all, and he had a tough time reengineering his mind to make decisions that were not biased toward prior behavior patterns in the market—as many of us do. At some point, nonetheless, if we are having trouble establishing new decision patterns, we have to ask ourselves one thing—how much longer am I going to lose money before I learn to change my mind? Once decided, trading will transform into another distinct landscape much more enjoyable to navigate.

Trading today's markets well suggests we approach the playing field every day without predisposition toward movement so much that it colors our ability to make clear, unbiased decisions based on fact. Contemplate how difficult that might really be if we are to do it well. No easy feat. When was the last time we made a decision based only on empirical data instead of our trusty preconceived notions? Most of us make decisions daily on only preconceptions, so changing our decision structure will be difficult, but most necessary to trade with precision.

The Macro View of Markets Should Not Be Traded

Trading markets well does not come from amassing knowledge best left for conversation over a coffee table, but I notice many of us spend a lot of time discussing these sorts of "grand idea" things. Traders have no business using macro-view information to form trading plans. Unless there is a 20-year investment plan in consideration, discussing macro events such as the potential of future political unrest, global economic projections, or how the world might change if we could develop cold fusion and then trading on these grand sweeping and momentous thoughts is a bit like whistling in the wind, or doing something else in the wind, so just leave that to Saturday afternoon barbeques, and put the thoughts away when Monday rolls around.

CONCLUSION

As we work on creating a strong foothold from which we can operate as traders, understand that the market is a fluid space, manipulated, but tradable, nevertheless. I urge the newer trader to keep in mind the following:

- Trading with mastery will take time and experience; no excellence comes without the time trading and watching the ebb and flow of the market.
- Our thoughts will create the impetus for execution for both entry and exit, so we should work on keeping them clear and unbiased.
- Those thoughts should be based on verifiable fact, not hearsay or opinion.
- Only useful information—filtered and in perspective—should be used to make decisions.
- If you choose to follow a trader you trust, make sure you understand the time frame he or she is cycling for the trade.

Simple mental checkpoints like these will not only keep us out of the impulsive trade, it will keep us profitable once we are in the trade.

CHAPTER 2

Technical Indicators I

MARKET POSITIONING SYSTEM, MOMENTUM, AND CANDLESTICKS

"If you want to be successful, it's just this simple. Know what you are doing. Love what you are doing. And believe in what you are doing."

—WILL ROGERS

My creation of a trading strategy and a defined system was the core reason for my success in trading. Over the course of three and a half years, I built the framework for this system on what I perceived to be actionable events to trade directionally. I decided to call it the market positioning system because I use it every day as my personal GPS for giving me clear directions on market movements and what my subsequent actions should be. After years of coaching students, it became evident to me that clear direction is the desire of every retail trader in the market, and because I have a heart for the lonely struggles that the retail trader experiences each day, having been one myself, I chose to share the simple strategy with those who seemed eager to learn it and expressed the dedication necessary

We won't address "why" it works but will just take it as a given and move forward with addressing the general formations.

Form and Function

A candlestick is formed by the range of prices that are printed during a specific time frame. When I use the term *printed*, I mean at what price the instrument (stock, option, future, forex, etc.) was bought or sold. A candle can represent a time frame of one minute or less to one year, depending on the time frame of the chart you are considering. Let's take a look at a basic candlestick formation in Figure 2.1. Candlesticks can be green and red, white and black, or any color you'd like to make them on your chart, frankly. Since we are in the black-and-white world, considering black-and-white options seems most appropriate. We will note here that black (or red) candles are customarily candles that close at a lower level than that at which they open—and white (or green) candles close at a level higher than at which they open.

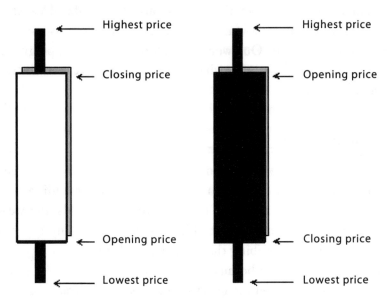

Figure 2.1 **Basic Candlestick Formation**

White candles show that buyers were more abundant than sellers—greater demand leads to higher prices. Black candles show that sellers were more abundant than buyers—greater supply leads to lower prices.

Keep in mind that charts illustrate the pendulum swing between supply and demand, and the fight between buyers and sellers. Each candle in our chosen time frame reveals the winner of the round (or time frame of the candle).

When we look at candles, our goal is to establish who has the upper hand in the time frame that we are observing, with our goal of following the side with the most influence. Because each and every candle represents a war between buyers and sellers, when candles begin to reverse their direction, it shows a shift in the power base.

Let's take a closer look at why I ask for a confirmation candle or the candle close before making a decision. Consider the black candle in Figure 2.2. This candle was white for a while. How do we know this? Where is the open of the candle? What color was this candle when it was printing prices in the region arrow 1 points to? White. If the candle had closed up there, it would have painted a completely different picture for us to consider.

How about the white candle? What color was it when the prices were printing at the arrow 2 region? Black. The moral of the story here is, wait for the candle at your trigger or alert points to close before determining what to do. When the price action moves down the candle or moves away from the top of its wick, it is signaling that the sellers have control and buyers are unwilling to pay more for the stock; when the price action moves up the candle or moves away from the bottom of its wick, it is signaling that the buyers have control and are willing to pay more for the stock. The market is *not* the place to root for the underdog; trading on the side of the weaker party is like munching on some yellow snow—not a good plan.

Real reversal candles have long wicks and close far from the low and high regions. They signify that the shift in power is swift and that the price point where the buyers and sellers climbed in was

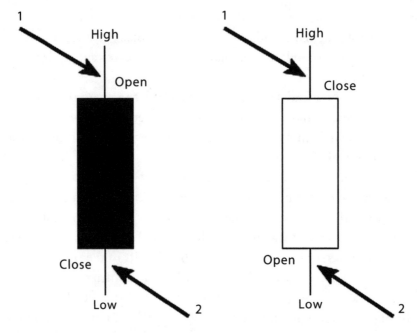

Figure 2.2 **Black and White Candles**

important. Keep a close eye on long-wick candles—sometimes they deliver critical price points from which we can trade.

Quiz Time

Take a look at the candles in Figure 2.3. Both arrows on both candles point to buyers losing traction and sellers driving the price down. However, buyers hold their opening support level in the white candle, and sellers break support on the black candle. Why does the black candle formation show broken support? Where was the open on the black candle? What might we expect to see here? Further tests to the upside, or tests to the downside. Mark on Figure 2.3 what might make sense from the struggle.

Where do we expect to see the next group of candles after the white one? How about the black one? Finding the answer focuses on one thing—something critical to trading—the hold and break of

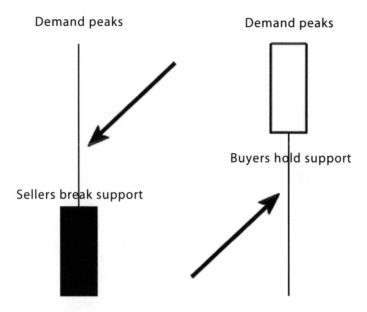

Figure 2.3 **Topping- and Bottoming-Tailed Candlesticks**

support. Therefore, we would expect to see candles printing higher to the right of the white candle and prices printing lower to the right of the black candle. If this does not make sense, it is essential that another walkthrough is entertained.

The Doji Candles

There are many candlestick formations that people study and use to predict movement. One of these very special formations is called the doji. A doji candle can be defined as any candle that has an opening price and a closing price that are the same or almost the same. This demonstrates a balance of power between buyers and sellers. It also indicates indecision. Since we know that balance in the market is a fleeting event, it is an excellent indicator signaling potential shifts or reversals in the market. Take a look at Figure 2.4.

Long-range candles signify a large range in price movement. They appear as candles with long bodies or short bodies and long

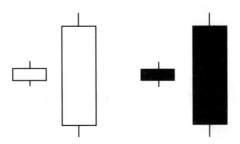

Figure 2.4 **Tight-Range Candles and Long-Range Candles**

tails—low to high—and cover an unusually wide interval of numbers. They signify indecision in the markets between buyers and sellers; if they are white, the buyers won the daily battle between the bulls and bears; and if they are black, the sellers won the day.

Figure 2.5 shows a doji candle. When the candles begin and end at the same price point, it represents balance and a potential tipping point in a trend. We'll watch for this with volume. Dojis become particularly important when they are accompanied by high volume after an extended run down or up. This usually signals a potential reversal in the near future.

Dojis are characterized by very small bodies, but they can also have long wicks (see Figure 2.6). Long wicks imply volatility or wide range of movement, as the long-range candles do, but with no clear winner at the end of the candle time frame if the price-range open and close is in the middle. As with all dojis, this formation signals a potential reversal in the near future.

Figure 2.5 **The Doji Candle**

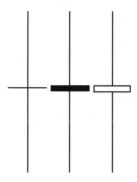

Figure 2.6 **Long-Wick Doji Candles**

The dojis in Figure 2.7 tell a different story. They show a shift of strength.

Let's take a closer look at the candle on the left. It opens at its high, and at some point during the formation, the sellers take control and drive the price to the bottom of the wick, at which point the buyers regain footing and drive the price up to end the day. The candle on the right shows the reverse. It opens on the low, where buyers drive the price high only to be overcome by sellers during the day who reverse all the gains made by their opponents. The days fol-

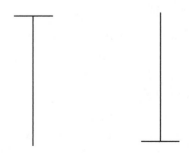

Figure 2.7 **Doji Candles Shift of Strength**

lowing candles like this are also very important, as they will signal the direction of future movement.

Reading Candlesticks

Those of us reading candlesticks in the fever pitch of the day often make the mistake of developing tunnel vision and only focusing in on *one* indicator, while ignoring everything else. Tunnel vision stands out as the most common downfall of the generally well-equipped trader. Remember that candlestick formations are relative and can never stand alone to deliver a decision. Candles need to complete at our area of interest on the time frame we trade before we make a decision. I cannot even count how many bad trades I've made not waiting for the candles to complete their formations.

So, why is it that candles show us so much about our decision making? The real answer probably lies with the genius of that Japanese gent who gave us the candles in the first place, but why does similar behavior appear to replicate so much in the market? I surmise since we are all made of the same dust and energy particles, it makes us, for the most part, react to the same things in similar ways. Probably puts a kink in the minds of those who solidly affirm we are absolute individuals, but . . . oh, well. I call it the *collective unconscious*—most market people call it the *mob mentality*.

Past the Individual Candles

Though we can simply look at individual candles and make assessments, looking at a group of them can sometimes paint an entirely different picture than just one or two. Looking at a group of price prints opens the world of technical trading to the emotions and price thresholds of the players associated with the printing of the price.

Deliberation on the chart in Figure 2.8 shows that it is trending higher, though grinding. Though many of us understand this intuitively, we fail to articulate that prices overall are getting higher. When I ask students if this stock is trending, I receive tentative

Figure 2.8 **Candlestick Uptrend**

responses. To become a trader who is profitable and consistent, we must be able to articulate to ourselves *specifically* what it is that we are seeing, to delineate and quantify. Our internal dialogue must be active. A closer look at this chart shows a number of things:

1. The right of the chart shows a group of buyers showing up to drive the price to the top of the chart, the gap shown by the arrow and the continuation of upside movement.
2. The early part of the chart, or the left side, shows relatively sideways movement. We can draw a straight line through many of the candles, no sign of directional momentum.
3. The chart is filled with misdirection and confusion, lots of inside and outside days near each other. (Note:

If today was an inside day, it means that all the prices printed today were inside the range of the prices that printed yesterday. If today was an outside day, it means that none of the prices printed today were inside the range of the prices that printed yesterday.)

4. Many of the aggressive candles (long-range candles, evidence that prices moved far away from each other) are retracing or giving back all the gains in the future candle prints.

What else can be seen at this stage from the chart? Write some notes—see if keen observation is on board.

CONCLUSION

What candlesticks tell us is quite relative to their counterparts nearby; therefore, making a decision on one or two candles is not recommended. A wide-angle view of the landscape is essential to correct interpretation. As we continue to delve deeper into the charts, and layer the complexity, always keep in mind that the candlestick is an emotion entity—a picture of a tug-of-war between the buyer and seller, and there is a story to tell. Practice learning to tell the story. Cover the right side of the chart and attempt to vocalize about buyers and sellers and where the chart might be headed. If we approach the candles as a story waiting to be told, our charts will take on a new level of depth, and our ability to anticipate future movement will grow exponentially.

CHAPTER 3

Technical Indicators II

MOVING AVERAGES, BOLLINGER
BANDS, AND VOLUME

"No man ever wetted clay and then left it, as if there
would be bricks by chance and fortune."

—PLUTARCH

If we have ever traded actively, we may have wondered why it seems
like as soon as we enter a position, it runs against us. Turns out,
our minds, without the proper training and necessary skills, will
invariably make the wrong timing moves into and out of the market.
We all seem to rush for the doors at the same time—rushing to get
in due to our fear of missing the gains and rushing to get out due
to our fear of compounding losses. We should keep this information at the forefront of our minds, as it will assist us in trading more
effectively. Why? If we keep ourselves aware that we are prone to act
with the mob temperament, and that what we are naturally drawn to
do is panic and make rash moves that will turn out to be detrimental
to our accounts, we'll be able to stop the knee-jerk reactions. And
when we learn to make measured decisions, we are much more likely

to buy on the way up after everyone has just sold and sell before the rollercoaster takes the ride down.

It is said that as much as 75% of all trading on all the exchanges is done by machines, but let's not forget that those machines have been programmed by humans who essentially embed their decision-making skills (as much as they can) into the software. This simple fact makes the market much more predictable than we could possibly imagine. High-frequency trading and trading algorithms are friends of the technical trader, so don't complain about them. Our assignment is to weigh the odds in the favor of the most likely direction and act accordingly. Oddly, or maybe I should say, humanly, it is the phrase "act accordingly" that we have trouble with and is the primary reason we fail as traders.

Ever look at a chart and just say, "Hmm, looks like it is trending up/down?" Most of us examine a chart this way. "Yeah, I see that. Lots of white/green candles, trending up. Moving averages are up; Bollinger bands are up. Yup, looks like a good long trade." So after some arbitrary time of looking at the chart, we decide to enter and buy the stock. Trading this way, though it can give us success if we hold for an extended time if the stock is generally trending up or if we are just plain lucky, is usually not a good way to make money consistently in the market. Remember, in the 1980s, that economist Burton Malkiel suggested that a blindfolded monkey throwing darts at a newspaper's financial page could select a portfolio that did as well as one carefully selected by experts. This, of course, could be true in a strong bull-market environment as existed at the time he wrote that. Only luck and the odd-man-out declining stock would make for poor results. Uptrending markets make the popular statement "a rising tide lifts all ships" quite true—luck sits with everyone. But depending on luck is what gets most of us in trouble, so we'll work together to rely on skill and not luck. Of course, if we are the type who happens to have a lucky star, all the better.

In today's electronic market, much more precision and thought is required to battle the competition. And, as I have mentioned, that is what you are doing—battling bright competition, something we often forget.

Most likely, from the dawn of time, we've never wanted to miss out on anything. If my kids think they are missing out on something someone else did or had, mutiny is on the horizon, to be sure. Because we are adults does not mean we have lost this elemental part of us; for some, it actually becomes a more pronounced behavior. This core "feeling" is the reason we will buy a stock if we have a favorable view or sell a stock if we have an unfavorable one. The reasoning is essentially the same: "*Wow*—I don't want to miss out on that move!" It makes us take the plunge before checking to see if the swimming area is one foot deep or covers a bed of coral for you to die on. OK, a bit exaggerated, but if you've been trading for a while, I am *certain* there are trades for which you would choose diving into a coral bed rather than live through the trade again. My goal here as we work through the details of trading is not to eliminate that feeling—that is not possible—but to temper it a bit with logic and a checklist. In training the mind to trade, we must set up some "train tracks" for our ideas to run on, or we will continue to career off into the canyon with our trades.

MOVING AVERAGES

There are many different kinds of moving averages, but we will discuss only two of them—the simple moving average and the exponential moving average. A number of people use the weighted moving averages, but I do not. The general notion is this: if the candles are printing above the moving averages, the stock price is trending to the upside, and if the candles are printing below the moving averages, it is trending to the downside. This is true provided there is a trend.

Moving averages measure the average price print per time frame. Here is what I mean: a 30-day moving average (the one you will see when you pull up the daily chart) collects the closing price for the last 30 days of candles, adds them together, then divides by 30. That number is then plotted on the chart after every single candle close and appears as a line on our charts. If we look at a 30-minute chart for the 30-period moving average, the calculation is made at the close of each 30-minute candle. Of course, this means that the moving averages will be different, for the most part, in every time frame we consider.

Though a little more complex in derivation, the exponential moving average does the same thing as the simple moving average but with one exception. Exponential moving averages give more "weight" to the candles that are closest, meaning these kinds of averages are more sensitive to recent movement. This weight is particularly important when a chart has had prior volatile movement but has since settled down. Overall, the differences are not huge, but they do matter, since we use these averages to keep us in our trades.

Moving averages are also defined as fast and slow, relative of course, but the premise is simple—the smaller the number defining the moving average (5, 8, 12, 20, etc.), the more sensitive it is to the prior candles, the more sensitive it is to change, and the more closely it follows the actual price of the stock. If you end up using a moving average that is too fast, you'll end up getting nothing but noise.

Slope

Here is something very important I want you to remember: *slope is everything.* We are going to be studying a momentum-based trading system, and without momentum, our trades will fail. Let's call it an *initial value condition* if we are in geek-speak, so that means, and get this one (I'm going to tell you, but you're still going to ignore the advice until you get tired of losing money): *if there is no directional slope, a good trade is not available.* It all comes back to that "missing out" thing. We think that if we get in before the move, that we're going to maximize our gains, and we'll catch the bottom (or top) and be delighted with our decision, except that either the move comes after you have run out of patience, or it never comes at all. Even worse, it could come in the wrong direction. This situation causes so much pent-up anxiety that it only adds to the mental gymnastics you already have to work on to trade well here.

Consider yourself aboard a wind-powered vessel at sea. If the sea is calm, still, or flat, how much will you move? Now, imagine a full northerly wind. Assuming you don't trim, where will you move? How about a full southerly wind? Where then? The wind is the slope: no wind, no slope, no movement. With a full northerly wind comes a steep upward slope; and a full southerly wind results in a steep downward slope. If you take a trade long and your slope is negative, you are facing a headwind that will usually stop you in your tracks, and the market will take money out of your account. If you take a trade short, with an upward slope, that, too, presents a headwind and sets you up to lose. Here is a rule of thumb: if your trade is positioned in the opposite direction of the fastest moving averages, you are losing money. This is obviously not advisable.

Moving-Average Crossovers

It is a common practice to trade moving-average crossovers. Though this method is a somewhat effective one, it is sometimes quite imprecise and can lead to significant diminishing of gains or increase of losses. Hence, we'll not use the occurrences of longer moving averages like the 50 and the 200 (like many folks do) to signal the entries and exits of trades for the most part. We will, however, notice the appearances of such occurrences in relation to how it looks everywhere else in the charts.

Our MPS trading system suggests using the 8 exponential moving average (8 EMA) and the 20 simple moving average (20 SMA), along with the 50 and 200 simple moving averages as general gauges. These longer averages are of use only to the day trader on the shorter 30-, 15-, 5-, and 1-minute charts or smaller and are of no use to the swing trader or investor, in my opinion, as we let profits really slip away waiting for a 50 or 200 average on the daily charts to trigger a move.

One of my favorite questions from as soon as I could speak, much to the disgust of my father, was *"Why?"* Sometimes, it's a good idea to answer these questions. So . . . why do we choose these averages above others? To some extent, these numbers are preferences that happen to work well with the MPS, but when we look at a chart, we often see bounces off these moving averages. These bounces most commonly occur at these familiar moving averages (10, 30, 50, 100, 200) because so many people watch these averages and anticipate a bounce that they will trade like one is going to happen. As more people see the trades, the more likely they are to follow. As you can see, there is no magic reason behind these moving averages. Instead, moving averages, as with most technical indicators, work as signals because of the perpetuation of their use by so many people in the market. This perpetuation is the reason for recommending the use of the ordinary ones above esoteric ones I have seen. Many black boxes, or automated trading systems, use the 8 exponential moving average, which is one of the reasons I looked at it in the first place.

As with all technical indicators, it is paramount to determine what you would like your technical indicator to deliver to you. For me, moving averages are a bit like barometers for the trade. They share the nature of the environment, and they alert me to change on the horizon, because when the change comes, the averages' locations relative to the stock will change.

Messages the Moving Averages Send

Moving averages will also send you a message about what is going on with the price during the trade. If you have fast moving averages moving further and further away from their slower counterparts, they are sending you a message that prices are in acceleration in the direction of the fastest moving averages, and as long as they are moving further apart, the move will continue. At the end of every day, take a look at your charts and just look at those moving averages. Are you seeing them drift apart, signifying acceleration? Are they parallel to each other, confirming a constant rate? Or are they getting closer to each other? When they begin to close the gap between each other, we know that slowing or deceleration of the momentum is occurring, and this should always raise an eyebrow if we are in the trade.

In developing a good trading system, thinking carefully about what and how many indicators to utilize is very important. The more indicators on a chart, the more likely it is that they will send conflicting messages, resulting in difficult decision making. As we move forward toward excellence in trading, take the time to bring to the forefront of your mind that more is not necessarily better. We will use a total of only five parameters in our trading system: the moving averages, the Bollinger bands, volume, multiple time frames, and the Fibonacci retracement levels. We've just discussed moving averages, so let's move on to the Bollinger bands.

USING BOLLINGER BANDS

It is my sense that many traders fail to succeed because they do not look at the market as an organism that can be pondered. What in the world does that mean? Well, we have a tendency to look at technical indicators as just numbers on a chart, triggers to watch—you know, that sort of thing. From here on out, I'd like for you to take the stance that the market is a person, or at least an emotional entity that gives clues about when it's going over the deep end, or overreacting. The market is like a rubber band that can stretch only so far, and there are places that it can stretch no further. The Bollinger bands show us how far the rubber band can stretch, by and large, and it has a tendency to spring back as soon as it gets hyperextended. Let's take a look at Bollinger bands and discuss what some of these formations show us.

Range of Expected Moves

If you've been trading for any length of time, you have at least heard of Bollinger bands. Many traders look at these oddly shaped bands and don't quite know what to do with them. Let's take a look at them from a general perspective with a little hint of math. What? You thought I would write a book and not squeeze some mathematics in there? If you know me, you know there's not a chance. But I do promise to be concise and straightforward enough so that you don't throw the book down and run screaming from the room.

Bollinger bands are sometimes called *volatility bands*. In simple terms, let's equate them to measuring the moods of the most even-keel person you know (small ranges of emotions) with the most emotional person you know (large range of emotions). Stocks are measured in the same "emotional" range, with each stock being most often a particular type—some being on a very even keel, like perhaps a utility, and others having wild swings, also called *high-beta stocks*. If you look at any stock with Bollinger bands charted, you'll notice that the bands move from being narrow to very wide. Narrow means the prices are printing with little variation, and wide means the prices are printing with greater variation. This indication of variations allows you to look at any stock and instantly determine whether it is in a period of active momentum or rest. Said another way, Bollinger bands define a range of prices that a stock may have the potential of printing—high to low—at any given time. How can we be sure that this is true? Because future price prints are relative to the closeness of the most recent past price prints.

For instance, if you are watching a stock that is priced at $150 at 10:53 A.M., it would be highly unusual if the stock printed $5 at 10:54 A.M. on the same day. It is more reasonable to assume that the stock will print $153 or $146 while still around the original time. In mathematical terms, it defines a "confidence interval" of prices. The default setting in most trading software is 20, representing the simple moving average, and 2.0 standard deviations, which will build a 95% confidence interval. The band produced says that with 95% confidence, all the prices printed should fall within the bounds of the band. Well, just a quick look at any chart plotted with these levels will show that they pierce the bands quite often without giving us a clear plan of action.

Like the moving averages, we use the Bollinger bands to give us clues to possible directional change or overall environment. When the bands define this statistical range that a stock price should print, what we look for are prints outside of the bands to alert us to the element of change possible on the horizon. Bollinger bands, also like moving averages, have slope. When there is observable slope in the bands, there is strong momentum afoot, but even when the bands are flat, they give us signals on the movement of the stock.

Clues in the Bands

For the reason I just mentioned, we do not use the default parameters that most technical trading systems use for the Bollinger bands. Because we use the bands to identify outliers, breakout momentum, and exhaustion potential, we want to make sure we set the parameters to identify those "real" outliers that cause reversal. The smaller the parameters used to define the Bollinger bands, the tighter the bands are. The tighter the bands are, the more likely it is that the parameters will pierce the edges of the band. That is not something that we are interested in observing, as we would like the indicator to do something that tells us it is time to prepare for entry or exit. It is possible to widen the band by using larger parameters so that if a price does break through the band (with a candle wick or body), we know with a high probability that it will generally signal a price reversal. If not a reversal, this break will at least identify the beginning of unusual movement. Using wider parameters, we also give the stock more room to move around, and we are less likely to get "shaken out" of the trade (given the false signal to exit). If day-trading, use the simple moving average setting of 25, with the standard deviation as 2.5; and if swing-trading, or holding for longer than a day or two, use the 30, 2.5 settings you will see as choices in your software. These are relatively standard on all trading platforms.

Let's walk through an illustration of these concepts. Take a look at Figure 3.1.

Figure 3.1 shows us a number of things that Bollinger bands reveal. Arrow 1 displays evidence in the chart of upside momentum. The candlesticks are all printing above the midline and close to the band. Just above this momentum, we see strong acceleration of this momentum with broad volume increase. Though a pierce of the band normally signals reversal, steep movement like this in which buyers are rushing in defies that general rule of thumb. Arrow 2 shows sideways action after steep acceleration. Notice how the bands inflect and change direction just above this sideways pricing behavior. Changes like this signal the disappearance of momentum or possible reversal and should be monitored. Notice how close the bands are together at arrow 3. This occurs when the volatility or movement of price slows down significantly. The tight range of price prints will make the bands very tight. This waisting is called a *volatility squeeze*. This formation is extremely helpful in identifying high-probability trades, as they can never stay so tight—they must expand, and that expansion event will give us the

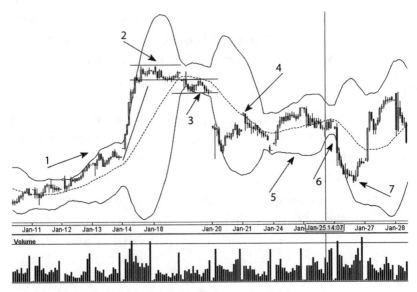

Figure 3.1 **Bollinger Band Formations**

trade. Arrow 4 highlights the failure of the stock to breach prices above the midline of the bands, and this generally suggests weakness and more downside movement, while arrow 5 shows real stock indecision by the appearance of a relatively flat moving average, flat bands, and the stock moving from the bottom to the top of the bands. Arrows 6 and 7 reveal what breakdown acceleration looks like in the beginning and what it looks like at inflection and reversal at the end, respectively. Notice how arrow 7 draws attention to the lower price that prints away from the band—this is always a sign of slowing.

THE BUSINESS OF VOLUME

Volume is an important technical element of trading. I call volume the "excitement" factor. To newer traders, the concept of volume is sometimes alien, and we forget that it is usually an extension of the price favor. Here's a simple example to illustrate the point. Let's say we see a print (purchase or sale) of $51.50 in a stock that has been moving up very well; as a matter of fact, let's say it is a new high for the day. If we are trading a breakout, meaning the new higher price signals that upward movement is afoot, we would most likely initiate an order to buy here. However, let's say that the number of shares that went at $51.50 is 100. Ponder the question for a moment—how important is that order in the grand scheme of the market? Does that imply in any way that the stock has many interested buyers who will drive the price up? Of course, it does not. The heavier the volume appears in a stock, the more likely it is in continuation of new price discovery and acceleration in the general direction.

For this reason, volume is extremely important to consider when trading. If you do not focus on the volume of transactions at a particular price, you will often find yourself on the wrong side of the trade, even if you are trading on your specific trigger. As we move along in our study together here, we'll see that a certain number of mental and physical checkpoints need to be established prior to taking a position. One of those is whether you have considered volume in your decision making.

Let's consider volume from a commonsense perspective: you've been watching a stock climb for a while, thinking about entering, while it continues to move higher. As the stock price moves higher, fewer and fewer transactions take place. This situation implies that fewer people are willing to pay the higher prices and eventually all the people who were willing to buy as the price moves up will disappear.

People waiting to buy a stock as it moves higher represent the demand for the stock, and as demand wanes, the stock price will eventually stall and reverse. By the same token, if you are shorting a stock (which few investors do as our minds really aren't built to be comfortable thinking about investing in something going down), and the price continues down but the volume decreases, fewer people are willing to sell the stock at the lower prices. The people waiting to sell the stock represent the supply of the stock in the market, and the more supply there is, the lower the price will be. Though there are many considerations with price settings as there is always a third party between the buyer and the seller called the *market maker*, what happens with volume remains the same. The heavier the volume in one direction, the more likely it is to follow in that direction.

What makes the prices peak or stall is a concept called *value pricing*. Value represents the price point at which the seller gets the most value and the price point at which the buyer gets the most value. These prices will create reversal points as we swing from one end of value buying to one end of selling value, like a pendulum. The market as a whole, and as a sum of its parts, swings from one end to the other with balance between market forces appearing for only a fleeting moment before either the buyers or sellers assume control. Let's consider this setup in terms of supply and demand. In most clean terms, it is not actually that supply and demand changes but that the desire to provide the supply or demand shifts price in the market. This is true because there is a constant level of stock out there (unless an offering comes to market—meaning the company issues new stock to be sold on the exchanges). So as the level of stock does not change, we are not really dealing with supply and demand in the pure economic sense.

Volume can be used as a pressure and temperature gauge. We need to look for these formations: inclining volume, declining volume, and volume spikes. Let's take a look at the following figures. Figure 3.2 shows there are more interested buyers still coming into the market.

Fewer sellers are coming into the market in Figure 3.3.

Fewer buyers are coming into the market in Figure 3.4.

Fewer sellers are coming into the market in Figure 3.5.

As long as we keep our eyes on volume when we make our decisions, we'll have a greater chance of getting into the right side of the trade, or the trade that is most likely to continue in the direction of our trade. The goal of the trader is to ride from one value level to the other—buying at the best value and selling at the best value. But as with everything in the market, it is not that simple, as those value prices will shift between time frames observed, so let's get an introduction to time-frame analysis.

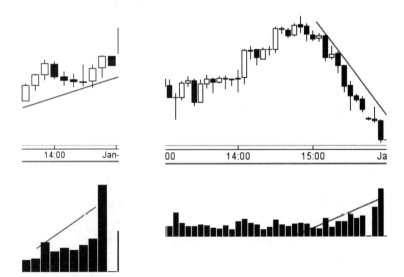

Figure 3.2 **Inclining Volume, Inclining Price**

Figure 3.3 **Inclining Volume, Declining Price**

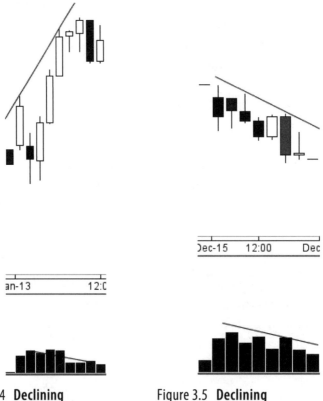

Figure 3.4 **Declining Volume, Inclining Price**

Figure 3.5 **Declining Volume, Declining Price**

LOOKING AT THE DIFFERENT TIME FRAMES

Take a look at the chart in Figure 3.6, and then compare it to the one in Figure 3.7.

The same stock is shown in these two charts, only it is observed during different time frames. Figure 3.6 is a chart of daily period candlesticks, while Figure 3.7 is of hourly period candlesticks. Consider how different the story is portrayed from each picture. If we are trading a trend, this muddies the water significantly. So, which direction do I trade? What is the real direction of the stock? Even if we consider ourselves advanced traders, we bump into the quandary of directional strength. We'll discuss this in greater detail in later

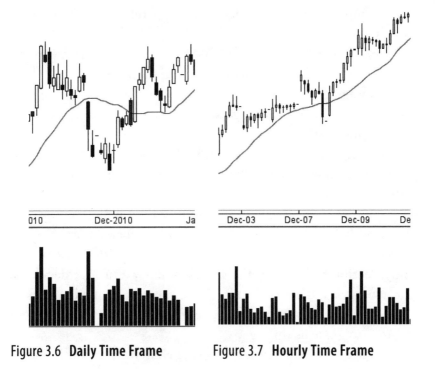

010	Dec-2010	Ja

Dec-03	Dec-07	Dec-09	De

Figure 3.6 **Daily Time Frame**   Figure 3.7 **Hourly Time Frame**

chapters, but let's consider a major reason that trades seem to go bad for us.

Many unsophisticated traders do not determine the appropriate time frame to trade. Plenty of us who approach the markets in this manner will buy or sell without regard to length of time we may hold our stock. This comes from these *false* notions:

- What comes down should recover.
- What goes up will continue to go up.

These two thoughts will keep the trader in trades long after we should have left. Precision trading always has the element of time associated with it. So many of us have entered trades without time parameters and watched them go against us without any idea of when to get off the train. By using a time frame, however, we can choreograph our trade in unique strategies relative to the time we are watching.

Since entire books are written solely on the topic of time frame, I would like for us to tighten our focus on the aspect that will drive us to our end goals of success more quickly. The *first thing* we need to do when we are considering a specific trade is to determine which time frame we will trade. Here is the rule of thumb—the longer the candle period, the stronger the trend. It is most advisable to isolate trades with time frames telling the same story in order to have a successful trending trade.

Multiple time frames representing daily candles, hourly candles, and half-hour candles show the same general story: they all identify the same trend that allows us to trade with confidence in the direction revealed by the charts—once we further decide on the appropriate triggers. Determining the time frame in which to take our trades defines a solid framework for the parameters of our strategy to guide us through.

When we take the time to view our charts across time frames—the daily, hourly, and smaller ones—we can see the strength of a move and make a choice for position size and length of position hold. In the ideal setup, different time frames should tell us the same story—either primarily trending up or trending down. The more selective we are about finding charts that are in agreement, the greater the chance of trading success. Different stories illustrate crosscurrents in the charts, and crosscurrents cause reversals that will challenge our premise for the trade, leaving the door open for second-guessing and a shake-out (meaning we leave too early).

CONCLUSION

Technical indicators in and of themselves do nothing more than paint a picture of the past. When we use them to draw a picture of the future, they become much more powerful tools. This is the way we use the indicators that we have chosen here, the moving averages, Bollinger bands, and volume. The most difficult thing a trader has to do is decide on a course of action, and being thoughtful about what the charts are telling us that might happen about the future is not as cut and dried as it might seem, especially if the indicators disagree with each other.

Following are some key points to keep in mind:

- Learning to weigh what might be the best action only comes with experiences trading in the market—though there are some strong guidelines the trader should follow with these tools at our disposal.
- Moving averages, though reviled sometimes for their simplicity, remain one of the most powerful directional indicators we have at our disposal, and they should be given precedence above others in our MPS trading system as it relates to momentum. Nothing we use tells us more about directional movement.
- Volume will reveal the strength and likelihood of continuation of the move.
- Bollinger bands often hint at the type of strategy we should prepare for the moves ahead.
- The linchpin is often the time frame of the trade. Critical to a move being successful is the knowledge that the preferred move will last longer than just a few moments, and matching overall direction across time frames will be a key element of success in any trade.

Keeping our eyes fixed on the importance of these elements will make for much easier trading days.

CHAPTER 4

Trading Well Is Not Only About Trading Systems

"We must become the change we want to see."

—MAHATMA GANDHI

Trading well is about making good decisions accurately and rapidly while knowing when to change your mind or stick to your guns.

An analogy for consideration:

Why is it that I can understand the game of football incredibly well and yet have a snowball's chance in summer of getting superior playing results? Answer: talent, knowledge, decision-making skill, and execution of a practiced plan and strategy—and all of that sits squarely on my shoulders. Have you seen my shoulders? I'm not built for football.

Knowing how to trade, the rules of entry and exit, and physically trading well are two different things. Perhaps this is for the same reason that some people make great coaches but only fair players. Consider the stellar quarterback: he is prepared; he has practiced; he has studied his opponents; he is ready. He has a strong understanding of the landscape, scanning the field for the most open receiver. The movements on the field are swift, dynamic, ever changing, and never happen *exactly* the same way twice. What is the same, however, is the strategy, the routes each receiver may take based on the play called. Even these plans change if the receiver is thinking about losing the hands of stone following him. The quarterback understands this entire situation, and he's waiting for the moment he can release the ball, knowing where his receiver should break and get the reception.

To trade well on the trading field, we must be the competitive professional quarterback. Though we may know a system well, we work in a moving landscape and are constantly challenged by the number of decisions that are required of us in a trading day. The best quarterback will choose the most open receiver who has the highest probability of success, and so should we.

Buying one of those off-the-shelf trading systems that touts automatic success and worry-free trading will never deliver the success of the skilled trader in the "zone." Those systems entertain too much risk and are far too imprecise. It is the human power of discretionary decision making that creates the skilled trader. Unfortunately, we ignore this discretion when we first get to trading, thinking that our decision-making ability is spot-on; it took us to where we are now, and that's all there is to it. That mindset, of course, turns out to be wrong.

The "me" factor is largely ignored by most of us because, well . . . we'd rather blame failure on something else rather than our personal execution. No one *loves* to take the blame for anything.

THE TRADING GAME

Trading is a bit like this. We are playing a game where we have, let's say, three doors from which to choose. Behind the first door is a man wearing a set of brass knuckles, and he's waiting to deliver a shot to the face; the second door is our brokerage firm, which will take a transaction fee for simply opening then closing the door; and

the third is a lovely knapsack full of Benjamins. Every time we open a door and close it, our items shift around between doors. We do not quite know where our sack of cash went, like a shell game. We have a system, the MPS, of choosing doors that is relatively reliable if expertly executed, 75% or so, and we understand it fairly well. Since the MPS carries the success probability of 75%, there is a 25% chance that we do not choose the correct door.

We take the leap, and according to our system rules, this time we choose door number one. We open the door only to see emptiness at first, but as we peer inside, flying out from the left comes our brass-knuckled present giving us a stinging blow to the head. We quickly retreat. Thus begins the mental reevaluation event, when we make excuses or think "the market is rigged," "this system stinks," or "good grief, could I get a little luck here, huh?" These thoughts invariably take our mind off the system, but when we refocus, we find that our system has isolated door number one again. If we put ourselves in this situation viscerally, do we actually want to open door number one again? I'm going to go ahead and answer for myself: *no!* Trading turns into fearful business quickly with losses or surprises, and we must constantly fight this internal battle to come out ahead against our competition.

Because things are shifting constantly behind the doors, what might sit behind door number one could be the knapsack or the broker or "Knuckles," as we'll call him. So as we muster up the courage to move again after the system has told us to—we open the door, but later than we should have, and there's Mr. Broker fleecing our pockets. Only after repeated attempts at the doors, using our system, acting quickly, and leaving as required, do we pick the knapsack more times than either of the other two potential outcomes.

If we choose to day-trade or to swing-trade versus invest long term in the market, the scenario just described is a large measure of our daily existence, and how we fare has far more to do with our abilities to follow direction, address fear, and manage our exposure than any system out there. So how do we prepare ourselves mentally at the outset to trade the market?

THE PREMISE

There are some important factors we must take into account when we enter the market, obvious truths that many of us fail to consider. Every trade we'll ever make is our entry into a competition, a competition between a buyer and a seller. We will either win or lose, relative to the specific trade. As retail traders, we would be wise to remember that we are competing against world-class organizations and institutions, against the best and brightest people and machines. Most of us come to trading with a tricycle thinking we can race Lance Armstrong and have a chance of winning. *Never forget who your competition is.* Prepare accordingly. Realize that we work on a shifting playing field and we must learn to shift with it. This fact is the first thing we need to take on board and mentally accept before we have a chance of becoming a consistent performer in the market.

We also need to accept the fact that no trading system is right all the time, and because of that, we will be wrong sometimes in our direction to trade, even when we do everything right. Being wrong is just part of the game; how we prepare to meet those times is directly related to our account balance. Hesitating takes the best trades away from us, and in the time we wait, the knapsack gets replaced by Knuckles, the physical and mental wrecking machine. View each trade strategically—exposure and risk versus reward. This is the essence of solid money management, and only proper money management will keep you in the game long enough to learn it. The question of whether we can keep more money than we lose can only be answered by how well we manage risk (which we will discuss in detail in Chapter 5). Before we move forward, though, let's take a minute to look at a major issue all traders inevitably combat: fear.

HOW TO TRIUMPH OVER FEAR

Benjamin Franklin said, "Do not fear mistakes. You will know failure. Continue to reach out." Fear and trading typically go together for us like peanut butter and jelly—we hardly seem to see one with-

out the other. Unfortunately, most of the time fear tastes like orange juice after toothpaste. We have to separate fear from trading and replace it with the knowledge we can execute a plan, no matter what.

Uncertainty Is the Petri Dish of Fear

It's a story of circular destruction; uncertainty is the buffet that feeds fear, and fear breeds failure. More uncertainty, more fear, and more fear, more failure. The only thing that can conquer fear is faith. In trading, the faith is in our ability to decide correctly, believing in our capability and personal skill. Think about how true this statement is—we can see it particularly overtly in children, but we adults are better at hiding these things. Granted, some of us are far more confident than others, but each of us carries fear, and the cornerstone of all fear is uncertainty as it relates to how it will affect our well-being. It is my estimation that fear cannot be conquered, as it is too primal, but it can be replaced. We, therefore, work through a substitution event when fear tries to capture us, especially in the market.

Preparation and Planning

It is unfortunate that left to our own devices we would normally buy high and sell low. Physiologically, in the face of uncertainty, our minds and bodies tell us to cut and run. Often, the best long trades exist in areas we feel like selling, and the best short trades are in selling areas that we feel like buying. Using any system with a chance of failure always makes us nervous, so the first mental reengineering we must do is learn to operate in an environment of the ambiguity of the market. That's easier said than done, incidentally, and quite a few of us know this. As we cement the technical information in our minds, learning to choose the most lucrative of options will become much more straightforward. But just knowing what to do does not mean we will do it, as I have mentioned. So how do we make knowledge turn to power?

I watched the Blue Angels once, and I was struck by something fascinating. Turns out, the pilots for the Blue Angels all get together to practice their routine with their eyes closed inside a large conference room. They sit and listen to the drone of the captain's voice; he tells them where they are and when to move. They orchestrate their individual movements and events to the second of exactly what they're going to do. The goal is to complete their entire routine as if they were blindfolded. They perform this exercise over and over again, before they get up into the danger of the clear blue skies traveling at hundreds of miles an hour next to each other. The Blue Angels pilots know something we might not: this kind of preparation allows the body to respond according to the stimulus it experiences.

Many of us fall to a state of indecision when a trade begins to go bad because we have not considered one particular outcome or another in detail. When we trade, we're usually thinking about how much we're going to make, not what we have at stake, might go wrong, or *what we absolutely have to do so things don't go wrong*. A trait that is significantly different between the novice and the experienced trader is that the experienced trader always knows what's at stake and what to do when the train is about to derail. The inability to realize the potential negative outcomes sits in all of us in the daily movements of the market, especially if we've been trading for a while. The question is, how do we change this?

I'm going to offer one simple solution, but I'm also going to hazard a guess that it's going to be one of the things rarely practiced, though we know it should be done: visualize a trade going bad. This action is one of the most important we should perform, but we have trouble doing so due to the overall need for concentration involved. The suggestion is straightforward, but the execution is demanding. The question becomes, what in the world would you do this for?

If we know what's ahead, we'll be able to divert disaster—just as seeing the pothole in the road, and imagining just how dreadful running over it with those low-profile tires would be, makes us merge to the left. What if we didn't know what that pothole would do to the car? What if we had not been looking ahead and never saw it? We might swerve too quickly, overcorrect, spin out, and crash into the guard rails or the cement median. A lack of preparation will open a wide door to trouble. Trading well and avoiding common irrational behavior takes preparation.

As many of my coaching students know, I liken a trader to a professional athlete. When do most professional athletes work on their skills? During game time or before the game ever comes? There is something primal that happens when we find ourselves in a fix, and we either move to combat the situation or become frozen by inaction, typically acting too late and in the wrong way. We either choose to analyze, assess, evaluate, and make a decision—or we freeze, then cut and run. The first step in our road to becoming a professional trader is to eliminate this common fight-or-flight syndrome. Here's how we do that:

1. Realize that anxiety comes from a lack of preparation and knowledge.
2. Plan to prepare.
3. Prepare. (Too often we complete step 2 but never get to step 3.)
4. Execute the plans that grew out of preparation.

The problem is that most of us getting around to reading this book already have had a string of losses behind us. The ideal situation would be that we read this book first and then embark into the trading world, but unfortunately, there is a fallacy perpetuated out there making us think that trading for a living is easy. We know it's not, though. It will tax us emotionally, mentally, psychologically, and physiologically and cause us to doubt everything about ourselves. Trading losses can drive us to the depths of despair; trading wins, to the top of the mountain. I often wonder whether traders are thrill junkies or just plain masochists.

But trading is like golf. It's those tiny details that keep us winning or losing, the details that we don't know, the details we know we don't know, and the details that seem to be glossed over in so many trading books I have read.

THE MENTAL ACTION PLAN

As a day trader, it is necessary to assess your performance on a daily basis, reviewing your personal expectations to make sure they are realistic. The following questions will help you in doing so and should be considered before you trade:

- **Am I looking for a trading system that works 100% of the time?** If we are honest, most of us will answer yes here. It is natural to desire this, but trading is an unnatural thing. The correct answer should be no, and a "no" that you actually mean.
- **Am I comfortable with being wrong?** This is a major space of modification that we all need to work on as no one is truly comfortable being wrong, but in trading, we must know that we will be wrong, and we will lose money. Attempt to be comfortable being wrong and accept the fact that changing your mind is OK if our system gives us a new set of directions in the market.
- **Am I *afraid* to lose money?** This is a big problem for us. Nobody likes to lose money. If loose bills disappear in the bottom of my cavernous purse, I am disturbed until I find them (usually under the box of mints or a hairbrush). When we trade, we cannot be afraid to lose; it stops us from playing well. Nothing about trading should create fear, and I can pretty much guarantee that most of us who are dabbling in day trading or have started working in the market trade very fearfully. We can be anxious, yes, cautious, yes, but fearful? No. The great thing about losing is that we get to decide by how much.
- **Am I willing to understand that I will need to incorporate a new style of thinking as it relates to**

trading? As the adage goes, as you think, so you are, and if that is not where you want to be relative to the career of trading, mental adjustments are in order. It's as simple as that.

- **Am I willing to plan and act deliberately?** To have consistent success in this field, we must resist impulse movements. The United States is a nation that values quick thinkers, and we do need that, but deliberate thought is to be a much greater part of our success than the ability to think quickly.

- **Am I willing to do "homework"?** Most of the work I do in the trading world is done outside the hours of the market. I am able to look at the market as the playing field, like an athlete in a professional sport. I am all too ready to put in the work off the field. It is critical to success.

- **Am I conscious of the fact that my execution is critical to a higher level of success?** Finding the right trading methodology is important, and it must suit who we are, but if it does suit us, we still have to be in charge of our fate.

- **Am I willing to take responsibility for my positions?** If we are inclined to "pass the buck," trading will give us trouble. We must choose to accept responsibility in whole for where our positions lie. We cannot blame the market for our results, because in the end, we are the ones who chose to enter or failed to exit. This one is very tough for some of us, and I can hear some balking from that internal voice at that. I'm not saying the market won't deliver surprises and set us on the wrong side of the trade, but I am discussing the depletion of our accounts over time.

- **Am I failing to increase balances or experiencing a steady decline in them?** If so, this is evidence that we are doing something very wrong. It is not the market's fault if we choose to be an active trader. We hold ultimate accountability.

So we ran through the gut-check list here. Where is work necessary? Can you make a list for your own improvement? Use a trading journal (discussed in Chapter 9) to assist in the process. Don't stay in the same space as a person. Even if our technical acumen increases drastically, unless we change the way we make decisions—on criteria versus gut—we'll be fighting a losing battle.

TRADER CREATES SUCCESS

Systems do not make the success—but instead the trader executing according to the system creates that. There is no holy grail of systems. Granted, some of them are extraordinary, like the one we're about to learn, but none will come through 100% of the time. Our decision-making ability—something I will reference often—will guide our choices, and that power of discretionary movement can give a system even more power.

Play to win or don't play at all, and that means a journey to self-improvement, a trek to excellence. Approach each day as an opportunity to be a better trader than the day before, and being a better person will come with it.

We are the masters of our destiny and captains of our fate. We will adapt and overcome.

CONCLUSION

Holding ourselves accountable for our trading decisions brings the power of rules to the forefront. Here are some things I'd like to impress upon the trader as the chapter comes to a close:

- Preparation will slay many of our fears.
- Know thyself. Take the time to really answer those questions in our "gut check" exercise.
- As we come to know ourselves, we accept accountability for our results in the market.

- The market is a shifting entity. Rarely, if ever, do we see exactly the same scenario twice.
- This shifting entity is filled with competition, and it is fierce. Every trade is won or lost by an opponent.
- Knowing what to do against our adversary is not enough. Execution is what matters. Plan your trades and trade your plans.
- Serious preparation is the only road to superior execution.
- True preparation and planning involves the outline of extremely particular scenarios—not just the "one" we expect.

Once we learn a good system, it must become part of our habitual trading nature. That is tough without constant reinforcement, which comes from watching the system perform, testing the system's performance by observation and study, actively anticipating our plans to unfold as prepared, and acting accordingly if they do not. Expect to fail but never be content with the failure, and the more directed and focused your preparation, the more stellar your results will be.

CHAPTER 5

Trading Blind and Risk

"A blind man knows he cannot see, and is glad to be led, though it be by a dog; but he that is blind in his understanding, which is the worst blindness of all, believes he sees as the best, and scorns a guide."

—SAMUEL BUTLER

There are few things that bother me more than hyperbole or extravagantly exaggerated statements. One of these came from a touted billionaire giving investment advice. His words? Rule number one: "Never lose money." Now I know he said that back in the nineties, so I'll begrudgingly throw him a mulligan, but seeing that he lost a ton of cash recently, buying on the way down and selling puts that ended up in the money for nine months in a row, I'm thinking he might want to step back from that statement a bit, or if questioned, I am certain he would leap for some caveat.

Now, tell me, how in the world is that statement going to help us improve as an investor or trader? Here's another vague one, the grand premise is correct, and it leads into our conversation about risk, so I'll give this other gentleman more leeway: "If I have positions going against me, I get right out—if they are going for me, I keep them."

Here's what I've noticed. A *lot* of people in the market throw out "rules" that sound good, but in the end, they do little to follow them. I am a harsh critic of those who attempt to teach others how to trade with a *glaze* of what to do and what not to do all the time.

There is a lot of surface information out there, and I am thoroughly convinced that many traders with something to sell—a system, a trading software, whatever—try desperately to make trading seem simple enough that if you buy their products, you'll be a millionaire. There is absolutely no desire for most traders to share with people how difficult trading really is, day in and day out, nor is there much desire to reveal any "real secrets." I'm convinced if people knew exactly how intricate precision trading is, the rank and file yearning to trade would immediately be thinned. I'm not sure many people really want to learn that it is one of the most difficult careers we can choose, and getting back up after a pounding to dust ourselves off is a frequent habit.

GUIDE? WHAT MAKES YOU THINK I NEED A GUIDE?

Climbing is pure exhilaration; it is about about conquering, about pushing ourselves to limits far beyond our normal existence. Though challenging, physically and mentally exhausting, and all-encompassing, when we reach our target, there is no greater feeling of triumph ever felt (for me, anyway, but I've never won a Super Bowl or a green jacket). Not to mention the fact that every night we sleep after climbing is often the best sleep of our lives. But as with any excursion of this type, there are always sets of rules; and the more demanding the terrain, the more rules we must follow to keep safe, or we will not achieve the summit.

Inspired to Climb

A stirring independent documentary called *Blindsight* produced in 2008 centers around a young blind man, Erik Weihenmayer, and blind woman, Sabriye Tenberken, who sponsor and direct an expedition of blind youths to a lower peak of Mt. Everest. Yup, you read that correctly: a group of blind people heading up the most treacherous terrain in the world. We should ask ourselves why the first thing we might think would be, "What? That's crazy; blind people can't do that." We quickly put restrictive borders and confines on many things that have much wider boundaries than we could imagine— my world has expanded greatly since this realization and willingness to erase borders. But I digress.

Our blind heroine leading the group believed in herself, so much so that she went *by herself* to Tibet after the Peace Corps rejected her application, refusing to allow this rejection to thwart her goal. Sabriye's desire to help the discarded blind youths of Tibet was so strong, she was determined to go alone if necessary. (Apparently, from the documentary, it is a common belief among certain Tibetan people that blindness is a curse from the gods for bad deeds from a past life that is brought into the next, so blind people are often abandoned or treated as pariahs.)

Erik had already been looking to take people up the mountain when he met Sabriye. Together they came up with the idea to inspire blind Tibetan teens to widen their own boundaries. They sought out the best guides they could find to assist them through their expedition and began to teach these kids how to climb. I'm not sure how many children the team took, perhaps six, each with his or her own guide to climb with. Their target was the summit of Lhakpa Ri, about 6,000 feet below the summit of Everest but no doubt still a climbing feat for the average person, not to mention young blind people between the ages of 15 and 19.

OK, so why did I tell you *this* story? Me and my never-ending stories. . . .

I look at everything and try to relate it to trading. It is a habit I enjoy, and so far there are only a few things that leave me with a blank stare and an absence of analogy—brushing my hair, for one, and cleaning my refrigerator, another, in case you were wondering. So, I began to think about climbing and the markets, and my climb up in the markets.

When I began trading, it was like I was trying to climb Mt. Everest without an experienced guide who knew the terrain. I either followed novices who looked like they knew what the terrain was like, or I followed experts so far ahead that the ground they were navigating through was completely different to the ground I was traversing. New retail traders learning the markets are climbing a hazardous mountain blind—only most of us don't take guides. Seriously. I have never seen another occupation whose participants resist formal education, instruction, and guidance quite like trading. For the life of me, I do not know why. I'm not even sure why I resisted formal instruction. Still leaves me quizzical.

What if we read a book about climbing, then set off to climb Mt. McKinley? Alone! Doesn't that sound a bit absurd? We don't know how to acclimate to the real environment; we don't bring the right gear because we are unfamiliar with the land; we don't know when to be particularly cautious or fearless; we can't tell when storms are on the horizon; and we take long and unnecessarily complex routes to get to where we're going. We spend so much time tripping because we keep stepping in the wrong places that the travel is arduous.

On the way up, the ground gives way, we get disoriented, and the more we try to climb higher, the harder we fall back, and the more difficult it is to get up. We don't have the encouragement that our guides would give us, nor do we feel any sense of confidence that we possess the knowledge to get us to the peak.

Skill and Sight

When we are new and inexperienced to technical trading and the markets, we regrettably approach the markets like they are simple things. See if any of these are familiar to you:

- "I'll buy every time the price crosses above the 8 exponential moving average."
- "I always sell/buy the 50/200 moving-average crossover."
- "I'll buy every time the relative stochastic index hits 20."

in the market, so numerous, that when we learn "piecemeal" from different people and then combine strategies, instead of enlightened, we are snow-blind, disoriented, and confused about what direction to take. If a trader feels perplexed, it is most likely that she is learning different trading strategies without knowing these strategies are applying different tactics from different approaches. It is all too easy to end up with incompatible rules of engagement and execution that become conflicting and ineffectual out of context.

ESTABLISHING A LEVEL OF RISK

The market is all about specifics, not generalities, and there is nothing that sparks my ire more than seeing folks tout golden rules that really should be pirate's code—a set of "guidelines, really" (quoted from Geoffrey Rush, or probably known better as Captain Barbossa from Disney's *Pirates of the Caribbean* series) that are actually dependent on circumstances. Trading, as I have said, is a thinking man's game—we don't have to be particularly smart, but we do have to be sharp to win, and we have to stay one step ahead of our opponents because when we don't, they will take our money. We also have to firmly establish our risk and exposure.

Accepting risk and ultimate accountability is the cornerstone of good trading. Every day we choose to trade in the market, we open ourselves to risk, and we may lose money every day—some of us a great deal less than others. Remember that we *will* make losing trades in our career, but the hand of established risk will determine just how far down that ladder of loss we are pushed.

This conversation is one that goes quite differently if you are an investor as compared to a trader. Since many of us come to the trading world with an investor mentality, I'll start with that one first. We'll assume this $50,000 investor account is going to be aggressively managed, meaning a clear set of stops are in place. We'll assume 8% risk and divide our holdings among a few sectors for strength and diversity of portfolio. Many of us will use exchange-traded funds, or ETFs, for this, but we'll discuss this a

- "I buy every time the 10-day moving average cross above the 30-day moving average."
- "As soon as the price breaks above the 38.2% Fib retracement, I'll always buy."

Even worse is when we follow people we think kno they are doing into trades on the Twitter stream without rh reason.

I call these instances "trading blind": seeing nothing, on ing the step right in front of us, and not even knowing wh and this is ill-advised. Let me share something with you. brandishing iron to sear it into your brain. The words "every and "always" do not exist in the technical trading arena, or markets for that matter, so don't take the trade according to rule every time. Study the landscape. There is no *ultimate* ind no "this one works no matter what," and too many junior trad on the hunt for some simplistic way to trade the market. I will there are simple ways to trade the market, but simple and very rate do not go together *at all*, and you'll have to make the de which you will trade.

Many of us think that we can learn about trading from ing a book, watching people stream their trades, or even wat people in a chat room. That's like sitting in a room with a bun brain surgeons thinking that we are going to know how to per brain surgery. The market is complex, and disaster is always wa at the very spot some detail lies that we never knew existed. L ing to trade well can only come through active discovery and ticipation, which is why I urge you to participate in all the exer in this piece of work.

If we have been trading blindly, thinking that just the righ are going to get us to where we need to go and some kind of ge guideline to following trades will keep us successful, please be a that it will not. Trading well requires acute skill, and sight is a top of the list. Seeing what to trade and learning what to see are ical measures of trading. There are countless ways to make m bit when we discuss the baskets of stocks. The point of this chapter is not "what" but "how." Let's use five performing sectors, and in those performing sectors, choose one that seems to be consistently on a steady uptrend with controlled pullbacks and lifts, not one with a chart that gaps up or gaps down and chops around. Charts with lots of gaps will blow through our stops, which will get filled at market price if it is a standard stop order, and that can really decimate a trade as market price can be significantly different from our stop.

Division of Funds and Exposure to Loss

For sake of ease, we'll put $10K in each of five holdings, with the intention of purchasing our individual stock prices at entry printing $10, $25, $50, $100—having already determined the choices. This means at execution, we would be completely invested with our $50K and hold a full-size portfolio with an 8% risk threshold. How do we as the investor set our stop mechanics?

Each stock holds the same 8% threshold, which means an 8% move to the downside in this long portfolio would result in the sale of the stock:

- **Our $10 stock:** this is $.80, or 10 × .08, so our stop loss is at the print of $9.20, and at that point, we'll be stopped out to fall within our rules and parameters.
- **Our $25 stock:** this is $2, or 25 × .08, so our stop loss is at the print of $23, and we'll be stopped out.
- **Our $50 stock:** this is $4, or 50 × .08, so our stop loss is at the print of $46.
- **Our $100 stock:** this is $8, or 100 × .08, so our stop loss is at the print of $92.

A dreadful day of getting completely stopped out everywhere means we would incur a loss of a minimum of $4K. Now why would I use the word *minimum* here?

Here's a little something that many new retail traders do not know: a stop triggered does not guarantee that we will exit at that chosen price. If our stop price is $9.20, and the stock falls from $12 at the close of the prior day to $4 at the open of the next—guess what? We'll get executed at $4, and here the word *execution* works remarkably well on several levels. This is why I urge the choice of top performers in top spaces and a stable price pattern without gaps.

Here's a look at that situation. First, Figure 5.1 shows a stable price-pattern stock.

And then, in Figure 5.2, we see an unstable one—even though it is still uptrending.

Though both charts are trending upward, our threshold for stock movement needs to be much wider for the chart in Figure 5.2. Notice how deep the pullbacks are and how it retraces gaps. When choosing a stock, consider whether the stock has any bipolar activity. Stocks with gaps and deep retracements are weak and need to be avoided in an investment portfolio.

Please keep in mind we are only considering appropriate stops once we enter but have not set parameters for entry. We must use our MPS to determine ideal, then acceptable, entry points to tar-

Figure 5.1 **Stable Trending Chart**

get. We did not speak about stop advancement either, but I will say here that trailing stops are not advisable in any kind of stock with a beta higher than 1.5.

Reflect now on the day or short-term swing trader's approach to risk. It is my opinion that it takes much more skill to be a day trader than an investor, if the intent is to outpace the investor's gains. The investor has the advantage of not taking real notice of intraday movements and won't get stopped out by these moves, provided the stop has been set correctly and he keeps his stops fixed and rigid. The investor is not required to move quickly and often, only mentally manage market fluctuation, which means accepting drawdowns after a stock has made a significant move and keeping an eye out for stops and general market signals of broken trades.

Figure 5.2 **Unstable Trending Chart**

How the Day and Short-Term Swing Trader Does It

The day trader's goal is to move along the same track as the investor on the way up or down, but instead of only capturing the main trend, we seek to capture gains and use market motion to increase our profits. Therefore, the day and short-term swing traders are looking for the trending but can accept the retracing chart as a trading vehicle. The day or short-term swing trader must be remarkably quick on her feet, swift to recognize change on the horizon, not hesitant to move, and able to analyze data rapidly and access next steps in a moment or two—plus she has to possess the general skills that the investor has, the knowledge and consistent execution of a solid trading system. What the investor has the luxury of doing in a few hours the day trader has only moments for. Quite honestly, few of us have the skill to be a highly competent day trader—it requires an inordinate amount of mettle and nerves of steel. We must also be incredibly confident in ourselves and our trading systems in place. These skills can be developed, but it takes extraordinary dedication to an intricate craft.

So now that I put all of that out in the open, if a desire to press on still exists within, I'll move forward with capital allocation and exposure for the day trader.

I am not in the habit of being completely leveraged in the market during the day, though some may do this. I am not a fan of this for two reasons—we divide our attention across a large number of positions, or we are exposing ourselves to too much risk in one or two holdings. Most often, I use around 50%–60% of my trading capital out of my margin account at any one time. I do not possess the mental bandwidth to apply concentrated observation on more than three to four stocks at a time, and that is after years and years of training with the system. I would like to encourage anyone learning the system to start with one stock, catch the rhythm, follow the process repeatedly, and when it is cemented, add to the list. This also goes against the grain of the mindset of the investor who uses a bit of a shotgun splatter approach—some are going to hit their mark, and others are not, and I am willing to take the risk that the ones that do hit the mark will make up for the ones that don't.

Anyone who knows me knows that I am tentative to accept that philosophy, mainly because I just don't want to hold a loser while it is correcting. Instead, I focus on a sniper approach to a successful trade. The thought is this: if we can make the same gains using one stock as someone else can using five, why not just use one? As always, the devil is in the details, and how well we accomplish the plan and strategy will determine whether we beat the investor or not. I'm not pitting the investor against the day trader, but please realize that investor mindset and trader mindset exist across a great divide, and many of us trading are using the investor approach and losing in the process.

We'll need some charts to explain how the day trader should look at stops, and more specifically, relative stops. In Figure 5.3, you'll see a chart on which I have taken the time to mark support and resistance levels with which we shall trade. For our exercise,

Figure 5.3 **Support and Resistance Levels**

our day trader is allowing only a maximum of $500 loss threshold for the day. Whether this happens on one trade or four, the number is fixed and should not fluctuate. This is a very important point. Unless we rapidly assess where we have gone wrong in a series of trades, we must stop trading after we breach the maximum we are willing to lose in a day. If we are trading without a maximum daily loss threshold, we are being exceedingly poor money managers as day traders. Losing trade after trade is a sign of something being very wrong. *Stop trading* until the problem is isolated, analyzed, and properly corrected, or more losses will mount.

Again, we are doing the analysis with the unavailable power of hindsight. The point of the exercise is to see the consistency of pattern occurrence and how it has a great likelihood of following through to the unprinted right side of the chart. Again, for the sake of illustration, we have identified that the chart is in a channel and will trade from the top to the bottom. We intend to capitalize on this. If we look at the black candle beside our white one where we picked up the chart, we'll notice that if price is going to continue forward, it must break prior resistance of region 1. It does not, so we can say that it will either retest the region and move to the second resistance level, at 2, or make a lower high than the 40.63 area.

As it happens, the stock gaps down below 4, relative support. Why is this called *relative support?* Because it is nearby and not necessarily a key area that might have been identified by a longer-term Fibonacci. Our pattern is a breakaway formation, so the completion of the candle closing below 4 is a shorting area. Let's say we want to short below the price region of 39.18 (we probably will only be able to get in somewhere around 38.75 because of the candle movement)—how far is it to relative support? We would calculate that by the following: 39.83 − 39.18 = .65. But we won't be able to catch that number, so more realistically, we have 39.83 − 38.75 = 1.08.

Subsequently, we can take no more than 500/1.08 = 462 shares. Regardless of the size of our trading account, this is our maximum allotment, and it means we cannot enter any other trades until we shift the stop down, and that should only occur if it is a logical choice. How do we calculate this quickly intraday with the time racing from us? We note areas of support and resistance quickly and do an estimation of maximum size. Since our trading system does not advocate an entire size being placed at the onset of a trade, we can hop in beneath our threshold and add as the chart dictates.

If our investor had taken this trade with the 8% limit, the stop would have been $3.10. Our close monitoring allows for tighter specifications and less exposure to loss. At the price break at 5, we can add to the position and move our stop to level 4. It is at this time, when the trade is now operating with only half of the position exposed to loss as the first is now at breakeven, we can consider entering another trade. If we develop our skill at scaling, we will capture even more profit. At the break of support level 6, we can shift our stop to level 5—and here we are in a trade with a risk of loss now almost improbable. When the stock recaptures level 5, the worst-case scenario is that we leave with the second half at breakeven and .72 on the first half—this is without the strength of scaling.

If we pay very close attention to support and resistance and we wait for candle closes—wicks can be the death of us—we can do very, very well. Note that if we established the channel formation, we would have closed our position (or at least half of it) at the test and rejection of 36.73 and gone long at the breach of 38.03, with the expectation that it will test 39.18—where again, we would shift our stops up and add to the position on the breach in hopes of testing 39.83. The failure to test 41.47 or level 2 is a signal that the upward press is weakening, and we would close half our long and get stopped out at the break of 40.63. Total gains exceed 3.95 points if fairly well executed and 2.85 or so if marginally accomplished. If our investor had chosen the ideal spot to go long at the breach of level 5 support and had a trailing stop (and this is why I do not recommend them) of the 8% level of 3.10, he would have been stopped out at 38.24 (3.10 below the 41.34 wick of level 7)—gains of .21. Just say no to the trailing stop loss.

I should say that there was a time I proposed using this trailing stop notion. For the novice trader incapable of isolating proper support and resistance, this is a fair option, but anyone keen on developing real technical skill in trading must master this technique.

Does this take skill? Absolutely! It takes an extremely flexible mind to move from long to short positions on the same day in the same stock. How are skills mastered? Practice, practice, practice, and a superior focus on the details of the chart.

Pop quiz: which is more important to time correctly—the entry price of a position or the exit price? Take a guess before reading on, come on now. . . .

Turns out the entry of a position is vastly more important than the exit, because the entry manages the risk threshold. Moreover, very often we will enter a position that will go against us. But just because a trade goes against us does not mean the trade is broken. It might mean that the timing is off, or it might mean nothing at all.

CONCLUSION

We can trade with all the prowess of the best traders, but if we fail to manage risk, we're still trading blind. Why? Because we are ignoring the dangers inherent in the enterprise at hand. Here are some key details I'd like you to take with you from this chapter:

- The fastest way to the top is by finding a guide willing to show us the way.
- Outside that, we need to realize we are crossing precarious topography, and the faster we learn the landscape, the fewer times we fall.
- Managing risk is an orderly and methodical procedure.
- We must decide how much we are willing to lose prior to entering our trades.
- Once we decide on what we are willing to lose, we need to stick to the threshold.
- Stable trending charts that trend give us the greatest chance to minimize risk.

- When we run into trouble and make consecutive bad trades, we should stop trading and limit our daily losses.
- The closer we buy to open at support or the closer we sell to open at resistance, the lower our risk threshold.
- The better we get at proper entries, the more likely we are to take home profits from the trade.

If you can't string a series of good trades together in a paper trading account, it is incredibly unrealistic to assume you can do it in a live account with real money as the pressure increases exponentially. Practice paper trading and establishing suitable risk before delving into the live skirmish. Great risk yields great rewards—that one we hear often—but great risk also means great losses. If we don't keep ourselves in between the lines, we're apt to leave with a bloody nose, and if we don't manage parameters on what we can lose, we might well leave with a broken back at the end of the day. Let caution be the order of the day.

CHAPTER 6

Waves and Fibonaccis

"The winds and the waves are always on the side of the
 ablest navigators."

—EDWARD GIBBON

Trading momentum means trading with rhythm, and like the surfer, we need the patience to wait for the right conditions—the right winds making the right waves—so that we might anticipate the swell and catch the move after the crest. This is the true strength of the Fibonacci retracement, a tool that measures the swell and potentially identifies the crest so that we might catch the waves.

MARKET MOVEMENTS AND WAVES

If we are to be fine traders, we must be able navigators of the market. It is a comforting notion that if we are able, the wind and the waves will carry us to our destination.

Market movements and stock charts can be defined as a combination of waves, and like waves at the beach, they come up with force and pull back with force. When the tide is coming in, the waves moving up to the shore are more forceful than the waves that retreat, and when the tide is going out, the waves pulling back carry the major force, while the waves coming in carry less power, and so it is with a trending stock. Consider that when the tide is coming in, those waves pulling back are not changing the direction of the tide—and when the tide is going out, the waves coming in will not change the direction of the tide. Stocks move in exactly the same manner.

There is a branch of market technical study called Elliott wave theory, a rather complex, often obtuse, and in my opinion, largely unusable theory for the retail trader to implement, that describes the details of these waves. Highly theoretical and based on precise initial value conditions, this theory is not utilized by most active traders I know to create trades and is often seen in analysis of past market events. We are in the business of predicting the right side of the chart—the future—not producing after-the-fact analysis of the past on the left side of the chart. So all we care about are the nature of these waves and what kinds of patterns are replicated. For us, many of these details will only clutter our landscape, so we are just going to examine how they pull back in relationship to Fibonacci retracements.

Wave Identification

Figure 6.1 is a standard picture of a chart. This is one of our familiar formations, but this time we are going to look at it from a different lens: the lens of wave action.

Take out a sheet of paper or your trading journal and write down all the things you observe about the chart in Figure 6.1 based on what you know. Or mark up the chart itself.

Working on our powers of observation, we can interject common sense into what might be occurring in the move upward that we see. Are there spaces in this chart showing strong emotions? What about relative highs and lows? Where were a forceful number of buyers and sellers present? Though not a core piece of what we are learning at this moment, we must work on always being supremely

Figure 6.1 **Standard Chart**

observant. Want to take the elevator instead of the stairs to success in technical trading? Become observant, very observant. Of course your ability to observe only comes with practice.

In Figure 6.2, you will see the same standard chart as in Figure 6.1, but in addition to everything we already know, we've added the concept of wave definition and their inflection points, marked by the arrows in this uptrending chart.

From a technical perspective, because the overall chart is uptrending, all the arrows pointing up are *impulse* or *primary waves*, movement in the direction of the prevailing trend, and the arrows pointing downward represent *corrective* or *pullback waves*, movement away from the prevailing trend. This situation illustrates one thing: nothing goes straight up or straight down, so stock prices' retracement is natural (and this means that anxious element that makes us chase a trade should disappear). Anticipating the inflection points at the arrows is what the well-placed Fibonacci will identify.

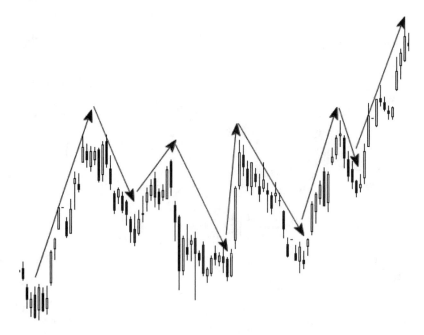

Figure 6.2 **Wave Definition and Inflection Points**

Fibonaccis are often placed in an area called *fractal geometry*, and fractals they are because waves appear within waves, and like patterns that replicate within themselves. The more we investigate the charts, the more we'll see that the measurements of retracement are always in play. Consider the chart in Figure 6.3, which contains subwaves, or waves within waves.

Think of the complexity that suddenly arises when we break charts up this way. If we look at the start point 1 to the end point 2, which of these waves is now the impulse wave, and which is the corrective? The chart has completed a full rotation back to its starting price so there is no trend. This simply illustrates that the longer we look at charts and work to understand them, the more complex they become. Isn't that the complete opposite of most things?

This is the difficulty within trading—the harder we look, the more we see. Our skill at throwing out what is potentially noise

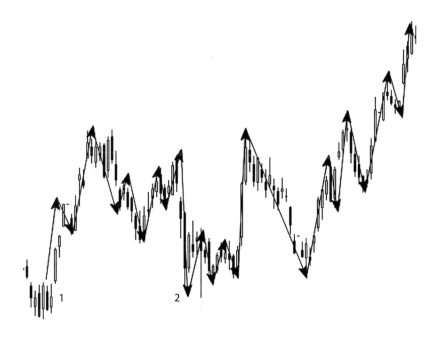

Figure 6.3 **Subwaves**

becomes increasingly critical to our success. For now, what we want to cement in our minds that we must first identify the waves before we attempt to draw Fibs.

Let's make this a bit interactive again. Go grab a pen or pencil and look at the following chart in Figure 6.4. Draw the zigzag pattern for the chart to see if the conceptual understanding of how to find these waves sank in. Start with the bigger trend visible.

Personal note to you again: please mark up your book here. *Don't glaze over on this topic, as it is incredibly important to manage; the nuances that only appear with active learning will escape you.* Trading requires interactivity and personal motion, specifically yours if you're involved, so use that pen or pencil, or this book will not help you nearly as much as it could if you engaged actively. Choose the largest wave cycles showing the ebb and flow of the chart.

tide coming in. The negative trending chart will identify impulse waves, which diminish the price of the stock, arrows pointing down, while corrective waves are the waves that lift the price, arrows pointing up, like the tide going out.

Trend Identification

It is important to grasp how important trend identification is in a stock and how that trend might look completely different based on the time frame. Here's something that keeps us out of trouble a lot: find a trade that is in the direction of the longer impulse wave for the most simple trade and most reliable trade. Trade the trend whenever possible until a greater level of competence allows for more strategic and complex movements. The trending trade takes the least amount of skill to come out on top, so when we are beginning or strengthening trading acumen, seek these out and trade them only.

I've been a coach long enough, however, to know that we'll ignore whether we see continuation or correction and trade anyway. It's the "This is it. I'm buying/selling the bottom/top, and I'll make a killing" syndrome that makes us choose countertrend trades. We only seem to learn by hammers to the face (some of us need more hammering than others), the experience of pain as a result of lost trading capital helping us along more than anything else, and, if we're lucky, we'll learn our daily market lessons. If we don't learn our lessons, we won't be trading this time next year.

Wave analysis is a large body of study, filled with geometry and proportion, but we are not here to become experts in wave theory. We are here to learn to master the art of trading. As such, all we need to remember are that waves retrace, and we are about to find out how to measure them.

AND NOW, THE FIBONACCI

There is a giant moot argument afoot. Do the impulse and corrective waves cause the Fibonacci retracements to appear, or do the anticipated measures of retracement cause the waves? Elliott wave purists would shudder at the thought of giving that kind of power to the Fibonacci retracements. Here's the answer: Who cares? Does that discourse get us better trading results?

When I ask people why they have never used Fibonacci retracements, they answer the same way: "It's too complicated," or "I don't know what they mean." Then there are those who attempt to use the Fibs incorrectly, coming to the conclusion that they do not work. Sadly, this response is customary for a trader who uses a technical indicator incorrectly. I'm not going to go into the history of the Fibonacci sequence because, for our pragmatic purposes, this will not broaden the knowledge base we need to become excellent traders.

The conceptual theory behind this sequence of infinite numbers is that in nature there is a hidden series of correlating patterns that can be measured by the sequence. This concept of underlying measurable patterns driving all design and movement of living things is the nature of the work behind the branch of mathematical research called *chaos theory*. How we use these correlating patterns to measure movement in the market, however, is based on something related to chaos theory indirectly: fractal geometry.

I see this term *fractal* misused a lot, and probably because I am a mathematician by trade, it particularly irks me, so I'll set the record straight. A fractal is an object that when split into pieces still holds the nature, form, and shape of the original.

Within the fractal space, we see the Fibonacci sequence—and in the market, we measure these ratios or percentages of wave retracement at the common levels: 14.6%, 23.8%, 27.2%, 38.2%, 50%, 61.8%, 78.6%, 88.77%, with 0% and 100% marking the beginning and end of the move we are measuring. These percentages measure the "giveback" against the primary move in our wave motions—the proportion of the move that is recaptured, or retraced. One of these levels mentioned is particularly important, the 61.8% level called the *golden ratio*. This ratio is also sometimes called the *divine* or *heavenly ratio* due to its ubiquitous occurrence and evidence of intelligent supernatural design in nature. The examples are too numerous to mention, but if it is of interest to you, do a "Fibonacci in nature" search on YouTube and plan to be amazed. From the ratio of our hands to forearm to the angstrom measurement in the DNA helix, the golden ratio can be seen in every single piece of nature.

Somehow, we introduced Fibonacci retracements into the market. Whether it is artificially placed, meaning if we didn't constantly measure and trade on these patterns, they would disappear, or a natural part of market movement is another point left to theorists. Sear to memory: "If it doesn't help me trade more effectively, I'm kicking it to the curb." Rest assured, however, Fib levels are there, attributable to countless algorithms and people trading at these levels. The challenge will always be whether we have the patience to wait for the level in question to test.

Fibonaccis tell where we've been, as they do in Figure 6.7, measuring the total rotation or giveback of the move upward, a complete wave retracement.

Figure 6.7 **Where We've Been**

And Fibonaccis can tell us where we are going—seen in Figure 6.8—based on the same calculations that told us where we had been.

As always, my goal is not to be exhaustive in the theory and application of Fibonacci retracements. That is another volume of work. There are Fibonacci extensions, expansions, circles, fans arcs, and time sequences—and though these are fair tools at refining the trade, I have found it does not behoove us to clutter our minds with these pieces of study. Let's take a look at examples of some Fibs and why we consider them well drawn. The Fib in Figure 6.9 measures from the tip of one inflection to the other.

We can define a Fib as accurately drawn if decisions of consequence or arguments occur at the Fib levels. What might this mean? Consider area A. Was a decision made there of consequence? Yes, of course, all decisions of consequence will be at areas in the chart that change the direction of the current formation. That was where all the buyers were waiting to pick up the stock. Look to the left of the 38.2% level. See any arguing taking place? Yes, indecision about

Figure 6.8 **Where We're Going**

Figure 6.9 Inflection Measurement

stock price and a failure to move off a region for an extended period of time shows up as this sideways movement signifying that buyers and sellers are in a tug of war—waiting for something or someone to be the one to create a price print (by buying or selling) that will become the tipping point. Moves off these regions are usually fierce and directional.

Fibs can be drawn from congestion to congestion regions around the inflection area as well and still be quite accurate, as in Figure 6.10. If a large number of retail traders who do not use Fibs play in a stock, some of the wicks are not as relevant as others at inflection points. Notice the way this particular Fib shows rapid rejection of the 0% and 61.8% regions identified by arrows. The Fib chosen for analysis must do a good job of "fitting" the chart—and sometimes that means using a congestion region, or high to low of a wave formation.

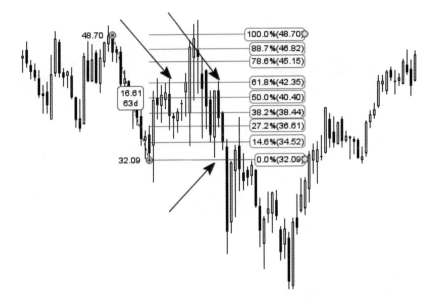

Figure 6.10 **Impulse Wave**

Assuming we are trading just the left half of the chart, we will label the impulse waves as those moving down and corrective waves as the ones moving up. The Fib drawn in Figure 6.10 is measuring the impulse wave, and the one in Figure 6.11 is measuring the corrective wave. Because the waves are interdependent, look at how well the Fib levels hold using the corrective wave as the area of measurement. Again, Fib levels holding means that there is either congestion or clear region of the levels. This continuous observance is distinct proof of the fractal nature of waves in the market.

Note to the more advanced trader here: I have also noticed that impulse wave retracements measure the projection of other impulse waves more accurately than corrective waves do, and corrective wave retracements measure the retracement of other corrective waves more accurately than impulse waves do. The difference, I should point out, is sometimes negligible.

Figure 6.12 shows a poorly drawn Fibonacci retracement.

Figure 6.11 **Corrective Wave**

Figure 6.12 **Poor Fibonacci Retracement**

The Fibonacci in Figure 6.12 is cut short and does not go to the area of inflection denoted by the arrow. The best Fibs come from start and end points at or near inflection. Do not draw Fibs from the high to the low of the chart if the high or the low is the last candle in your chart. This candle could very easily turn into a poorly drawn Fib if there is no reversal in the chart. Only Fibs measuring in between cycles are considered poor—all the others may be accurately used to trade. How we assimilate the surrounding technicals determines our movement. As I mentioned, the Fibonacci is not a stand-alone decision-making tool.

Fibonaccis, whether used by investors or traders, should be drawn using a wide-angle lens—the weekly or monthly charts—critical levels should be noted, and other levels not connected to the chart should be hidden or erased, whichever the software allows. The same should be done on the daily for the investor. For the short-term investor, or swing trader, do this again once more on the four-hour chart, and for the day trader, one more set of levels is required—the choice is between the one-hour time frame and the 30-minute time frame. Any more than that for the general momentum trade will confuse and clutter the trade rather than illuminate a path.

Note to the advanced trader—the only places that we should draw tighter Fibs come when we are trading the parabolic expansion or parabolic exhaustion formations—then individual candlestick retracements can be performed. If trading the futures or anything else that requires these smaller time frames like one-, two-, or five-minute candles, don't mark up the chart so much that a Fib exists every half point—what good is that?

Here is the key thing to remember about Fibonacci retracements: they measure the movement of market waves—impulse and corrective. To recap, an impulse wave is a movement in the stock that follows the general trend in the time frame we have under study. In that time frame, an impulse wave will retrace:

- To 38.2% before resuming the trend, if the momentum is aggressive
- To 50% before resuming the trend, if the momentum is standard and measured
- To 61.8% before resuming the trend, if the momentum is weak or unstable
- To greater than 61.8% retracement, and what we are looking at is most likely not a trend but a chopping, basing, or consolidating chart with no real measureable momentum and hence no trading edge as it relates to this critical element

A nuance here to keep in mind is that a corrective wave will be created by the retracement of the impulse move, but as it reverses, it means the stock is resuming the trend, that is, creating another impulse wave. This implies that a corrective wave is expected to retrace 100%, and in fact, if the momentum is strong, it will move to 150% and 161.8% Fib levels before another corrective wave begins. Don't lose sight of which is the corrective wave in a trend; it will allow us to pace our moves and to give the stock time to jockey around as we know a stock does not move in a linear fashion but a harmonic one.

When a corrective wave reverses, it will retrace:

- To 38.2% before failing its retrace, if the momentum is weak and a potential reversal is in play
- To 50% before failing its retrace and will hold at the 38.2% level, unless momentum is weak and trend reversal is in play
- To 61.8% before failing its retrace and will hold the 50% and then advance, unless momentum is slight (though it cannot be characterized as weak if it retraces as much as 61.8% and holds the 50%)
- To greater than 61.8% and signs of potential reversal or sideways action are on the horizon

Waves and Fibonacci retracements are inextricably tied together.

CONCLUSION

Though the argument rages on about whether one creates the other or not, the fact remains that understanding the rhythm of the waves will give us the precise points at which we can initiate the Fib lines and is the only place on which to focus our attention. Our navigation of the market rests squarely on our ability to understand how these waves move. From Elliott wave theory, there are all sorts of extrapolations we can make about wave forms, but working in the venue—trying to fit wave forms into the market—will color our ability to view objectively what is happening in the market, so I would recommend against it. All we need to do is anchor our mindset to the Fibs and the levels they identify and *wait for the formations to develop*. If we do that, the Fibs *will* deliver the correct projections when used with the indicators in our MPS and will deliver results.

CHAPTER 7

You Deserve Success

"In my wide association in life, meeting with many and great men in various parts of the world, I have yet to find the man, however great or exalted his station, who did not do better work and put forth greater effort under a spirit of approval than he would ever do under a spirit of criticism."

—CHARLES SCHWAB

Are we, or aren't we deserving of success? That sounds like the easiest question in the world to answer. Of course I am deserving of success. Here's a worthwhile exercise. Get in front of a mirror and look at yourself right in the eyes. Lean over into the mirror and bring to mind the most successful person (interpersonally or professionally) you've ever heard of—then I want you to say out loud, and loudly, "I deserve that level of success." Now, you know that I expect you to be active in this reading as it is the only way we learn, so I'll sit here and wait for you to do that. Sound ridiculous—try it. It is much tougher than it looks.

Oh, good heavens, just get up and do it, or the rest of this chapter will be vacuous to you!

Did you do it? Even after my pleading, some of you didn't (perhaps the more cynical of us considers this request silly), but the ones who did will create for themselves a higher level of personal achievement. Why? Because, folks, reaffirming that we deserve success is a very difficult practice. If we do not possess the skill of personal encouragement, we will not be able to stand the blows to our psyches the world will deliver, and we'll either turn into someone who blames the world for our woes or assume we are incapable or undeserving of success.

The first time I realized that I did not believe I was worthy of success was more than 20 years ago, and I clearly remember cringing. I surmise the reason I felt this way lies at the heart of my formative childhood years. Let's just say I grew up in a very demanding space. Sticks and stones hurt a lot less than words we take to heart. Who knows why so many of us consider ourselves unworthy of one thing or another. This probably needs an entire library of books to explain. It is a fact, though, that many of us feel this way. Oh, we say we deserve success out loud if people ask us; we wear a layer of Teflon when we are out in the world, but secretly we sabotage ourselves. Through derision, or believing what someone has to say about what we have the ability to do, or focusing too much on our failures, the habit of self-sabotage and self-derision is alive and well in most of us. When working with students, it is my experience that women reveal this on more occasions to me than men, but I consider that a normal dynamic.

At times when you are reading this book, I'll give you cause to cringe. It is intentional as if you desire to change your results trading, you must change what you are doing, and many times, that is also what you are thinking. Normally, it is uncomfortable to face habits we must change. As a trading coach, I meet a lot of people, and the hardest ones to work with are the ones who are set in their ways.

NEGATIVE SELF-TALK DESTROYS THE PSYCHE

There are those of us filled with negative self-talk over everything we do wrong in the belief it helps make for better results. I will tell you that it does not. I want you to think about the attributes of the best coaches around, perhaps the best coach you have ever had. Maybe they are firm, relentless, rigid, and demanding, but without their spirit of enthusiasm and encouragement to urge you along, your coach would not fall into "best" category. The best coach will sometimes tear you down but will be right beside you to build you up. It is the nature of change and growth. No one flourishes under constant derision.

Now, if that is true for the best coaches around, why should the rules be different for you? Unless a choice is made to retain a coach (as every professional athlete does, incidentally), you are your own coach, and your derision will not elevate you to peak performance. You will become what you affirm you are. I've spoken with many students on this matter. They seem convinced this self-disdain is how they get better. When I ask them to avoid it, they are resistant, saying that's just the way they process their mistakes and work on improvement. I used to think that negative attitude worked until I chose more constructive ways to encourage myself and found that this resulted in more success in my endeavors.

Treat Yourself as Well as You Treat Others

Here's my analogy for you—let's say you have a child or children you adore, and your goal is never to break their spirit or will but to guide them in the way that you deem best for their future. How will you approach them with mistakes or errors in judgment? Are you always harsh while reminding them of how poorly they did in the past? Do you deride them? If you do, take a breath and remember when someone spoke to you like that—then refer to the quote from Charles Schwab at the beginning of this chapter. Or maybe it is a boss or friend, someone you respect, whom you would like to help through an error in judgment? I would imagine if you are a decent person, not cutting and jaded by the world, you just might treat someone with care, concern, kindness, and instructional suggestion. So, wait . . . why again is it acceptable to treat yourself in a manner that is inferior to the way you treat others? Oh, yeah: it's not.

Mentally, you should not treat yourself as a substandard person, or you will remain substandard in the very area you outwardly wish to change. And if you do treat others like that, perhaps it's time for some growth there, too. Being better to others might actually make you treat yourself better, and you will become much more than you ever thought you could be.

You know what else this bad habit does? It becomes your ticket to excuses for failure. It's the "well, what did you expect out of yourself anyway" dialogue that feeds that part of you that expects failure, and so you will continue in your ways and use your own contempt to actually drive the behavior you desperately wish you did not have. This kind of conversation raises the blood pressure of many, but it does not make the information any less true.

Breaking the Habit

When you hear yourself in a barrage of scorn and contempt, learn to police your thoughts, realize them as destructive, and eliminate them. Most of us don't want to hear this, but you must actively manage what you think negatively about yourself—and others, really. Choose to be constructive, stepping through how you might avoid mistakes again, and find something to reward yourself with as you become better, not only at trading, but better as a person and better to yourself.

Those of us who grew up in harsh households might think that we actually do not know how to be better to ourselves, but we do. It is a conscious choice and a decision, a simple decision to shut the septic tank faucet from filling our brain with refuse.

AS WE SOW, WE SHALL REAP

Mindset is reality. It is proven over and over through scientific experiments that it is not that we are what we eat—but we are what we think. If our mindset continually tears us down, how do we expect to rise to levels of superior performance? Many of us have competitive athletes as friends or acquaintances. If we're privy to their preparation for high-level performance, we'll know that they do not allow negativity to cross their minds in any form. Whatever part of them that is related to success is tapped on mentally and expanded to fill their whole minds. This is particularly true of individual competitors.

In trading, we are all individual competitors, and our minds are our most precious asset. Why not take care of them like they are invaluable, instead of kicking them like a can down the street? We become what we think we are. Thoughts are manifested into action that defines us, and that is directly related to the negative soliloquy we grace ourselves with from day to day. I have a suggestion for you. Forgive yourself for past wrongs—and it might not be a bad idea to forgive those wrongs done to us along the way. As Nelson Mandela's character in *Invictus* said, "Forgiveness never hurts the soul. It removes fear; that is why it is such a powerful weapon. What is today is today; the past is the past. We look to the future now."

While we're here on the philosophy of reaping what we sow inside our minds, or karmic force as some call it, let's take a look at our personal interaction skills. Well, let's look at my interpersonal skills from younger days. A long time ago, and I do thank God it was a long time ago, I was a cocky, selfish, self-aggrandizing, brash, outspoken, often tactless, and cruel young woman. Wow, I really did not like writing that there, but it is true. Would you believe I wondered why a lot of nice people didn't like me? I had a friend once say to me quite heatedly, "You know, just because you're displeased with yourself doesn't mean you have to take it out on the whole world." (I'm paraphrasing—I've eliminated the expletives). I dismissed this comment immediately and told him he was out of his mind. After all, I was carving my way through the world, and I really didn't have time to be warm and cozy. I was busy, and I had no time for fluff. But as God would have it, I happened to meet someone exactly like myself in my twenties, and the horror of that truth set in. I realized I did not want to be that person at all. Interesting how we can see the faults in others so much more clearly than our own. Now, why in the world am I telling you this story?

Have you ever seen the exercise in which a leader in front of a group of people says to them, "I want you to turn to the wall and stretch as high as you can against the wall"? After they are done, he pauses for a moment, then says, "OK, now stretch a little higher," and the camera pans to the group and shows many of them able to stretch a bit higher. Of course, it begs the question, why didn't they stretch that high the first time? Physiologically, we can say that the more we stretch, the more we are able to stretch, but psychologically, the answer is also the same.

Waxing philosophic, I assure you that if you choose to be kinder and more gracious and concerned for others, the better you will learn to treat yourself, and the better people will treat you. If you're looking for people to be nicer to you, step out first by being nicer to them. You'll sleep better, feel better, be less anxious, and that karmic flow will follow you to the trading table. Contrary to what we might think, if we think of ourselves less, others will actually think of us more, and if they don't, the laws of nature will deal with that. Let's not concern ourselves with justice. Justice is always served in the very end. Garbage, you say? It is not, but suit yourself. There's a cynic on every stoop—that is your choice, and perhaps you'll be just fine without change. This is just my call to you to stretch yourself. Stretching really hard, by the way, hurts, but it completes the layers of foundation necessary to be truly successful.

Anyone remember why Emperor Chin was buried with his terra-cotta (and real) soldiers? Yup, he was afraid that all the people he had hurt and done wrong to would torment him in the under-world. Don't live your life needing terra-cotta soldiers.

ADDITIONAL BAD HABITS

Trading is a fluid and ever-changing occupation. If you are not adaptable, or adaptive, you will eventually begin to lose money even if you were making it before. The market has a voracious appetite for the contents of your brokerage account, and I recommend that you assume the role of guard dog before it comes to eat your lunch.

Dr. Robert Gilbert said, "First we form bad habits, then they form us. Conquer your bad habits, or they will eventually conquer you." Following are some additional key bad habits behaviorally we all suffer with—some in greater extremes than others—and some quick recommendations on how to address necessary change to help lead you to success.

Fear of Change and the Unknown

Oh, we'll talk a big game about change, but when it comes down to it, we are comfortable with routine. After all, the fear of the unknown is what will drive market volatility through the roof and send stocks crashing through the floor. It is the nature of our being. The way we bring this one into the trading world is by saying, "Well, I use the blah, blah, blah, and those are what I use." It really doesn't matter if that technical indicator stops working. We just think it will begin working again. This is faulty thinking, about as faulty as buy and hold since a good stock will always hold its value over time. If you need examples, there are a plethora of good companies being delisted every year. We are in a new world of markets, and it is so technically driven due to machines managing the flow that many commonsense relationships become useless in allowing us to define movement. But suggesting you throw out the things that kept us in the market for years simply will not go over well. Routine is necessary, but by no means is it necessary all the time. The fact is that being routine all the time shuts the door to innovative approaches and solutions. Realize you are resistant to change in every aspect of your life; keep your eyes open to it and ask yourself why you are resisting. Embrace change by gathering information; and if change is necessary to flourish or achieve greater heights, then make the choice to accept it.

"Right All the Time" Disease

I call this a disease a bit jokingly, but it will make your trading performance sickly. It is a very bad habit that will keep you in trades longer than you need to be. Being stubborn does not help you "make it" in the market. In fact, it often breaks you. There is no easy way to address how to work on this habit because it comes out of the core of who we are as people. Curbing overgrown personal pride will be a familiar battle to you if you desire excellence in the trading field. Either choose to face the potential pitfalls and triumph over them, or choose to fall back to where it's easy and you don't have to change. It's always going to be your choice.

Knee-Jerk Trading

By the time most of us get around reading books on trading, we've lost a fair amount in the market, the prevailing thought of "I mean, really, how hard could it be?" being the reason I suppose. Nevertheless, even though we desire to implement successful trading systems into our trading, we come with that impulsive state. The toughest thing a good coach has to work on is assisting folks to deny their impulses and trade in an organized manner. It is so hard to slow down and do it right that most of us give up on trying.

Struggling Against the Flow

So many of us who are drawn to trading have the maverick mentality. We either root for the underdog or go against the flow. In the market, unless you are managing billions or know a lot about market manipulation techniques (which tend to be frowned upon by the three-letter entities—SEC, FBI, etc.), we are served much better by following, rather than by leading. Don't rush for the front of the line; be content to be a follower near the front of the line. Your account balance will reward you.

Procrastination

This one is a killer. "I'll start a journal tomorrow," or "I'll look over my trades another day," or "I'll get organized next month," or a dozen other thoughts we have postpone our fixing the bad habits we might have surrounding diet, exercise, or something else we want to change.

Whitewash-the-Fence Syndrome

This is a particularly difficult habit to break because it is part of how we organize and categorize the world. But it is also the anchor of prejudice and unjustified bias—and it can drive a trading career to ruin. We are always looking for that holy grail. It's the desire to say, "every time I see this, then I do this," but regrettably, there is *nothing* in the market that follows exactly the same patterns every time. This might make us nervous if we really ponder the reality of that statement, especially since we have committed to the task of mastering the world of technical trading, but consider how many times we have to adjust what we expect based on a series of combined observances.

Here's what I mean by everyday shifting decisions. You step outside on a sunny fall day, feel a fierce wind, look to the far western sky filled with dark clouds rolling in, and walk back inside to grab a rain jacket since you'll be out for hours. If you were going to be outside for 10 minutes, would you grab the rain jacket? Probably not. What if there were no breeze or perhaps no clouds? Probably not. It is the combination of events that cause the adaptation of choice.

Lack of Attention to Detail

Think you're detail oriented? Yeah? Try to mentally recall your medicine cabinet, or perhaps your kitchen pantry or refrigerator. What's on the third shelf from the top, two positions to the right of the left side of the pantry/cabinet/refrigerator wall? You go in there all the time. Why don't you know? Because you and I filter our surroundings according to a focus of purpose. If we're going to look for aspirin, or olives, we'll overlook other things. (If you do know exactly where these items are, let me stop right here and applaud you—you are in a rare crowd. Or maybe you're like me, and you have a very specific place for everything, and it has been so for a long time.) The same thing happens in trading. We focus on one thing, ignore other critical elements, and miss the real triggers to enter or exit.

Success is a moving target, isn't it? What we call success in our twenties we might not consider success at all in our sixties. For each of us, a decision needs to be made to quantify this target at this time of our lives. So whip out that trusty journal and write some bullets, things that would deem you successful in your own eyes, not the eyes of others—*your own*. Once complete, turn to survey your habits; see which firmly stand in the way to your goals.

CONCLUSION

All habits can be broken—all. Some just take more determination than others. Our study of the trading system will work wonders to conquer that fear of the unknown, the knee-jerk trading trouble, and the whitewash syndrome, but for the others, add them or other bad habits you know that affect your trading to your journal. Choose one a week to work on them, one at a time. Face them and conquer them. Maybe you're not sure if you have some of these habits. Sometimes, it is difficult to do a personal evaluation objectively. Consider engaging a friend or significant other to assist you in addressing some of these topics; a surprise usually waits for us here as we are rarely seen the way we think we are. Don't be afraid to look at yourself and begin to grease the squeaky wheels, those parts of you that might need a little polish, so that you are able to claim the success that you deserve.

CHAPTER 8

From Simple to Complex: Long Trade

"It ain't what you don't know that gets you into trouble.
It's what you know for sure that just ain't so."

—MARK TWAIN

Trading techniques can move from simple to complex. The best way to learn them is by observing them alone, determining where the real strength of the technical occurs, and keeping that in your crosshairs. What we'll do in the next four chapters is walk through simple trading techniques and move to more complex topics as we develop skill. We'll work on a long trade, a short trade, and a trade we have no business being in—adding to our analysis our learned skills to outline the parameters for each entry and exit according to technical indicators and our subsequent decisions. Precision and attention to detail will always lead to greater profits.

THE LONG-TRADE WALKTHROUGH

We'll begin with the moving averages and general trends. Consider the chart in Figure 8.1 we'll be trading.

In the spirit of interactivity as it promotes learning, using the white space we have here around Figure 8.1, jot down answers to these questions:

1. What is the general trend?
2. What do you observe about the size of the pullback noted at the top right of the chart?
3. What can you say about the nature of the candle formations at the top right compared to the ones in the middle of the chart?
4. What direction would the most reliable trending trade be?

Figure 8.1 **Base Chart**

I will repeatedly impress the need for you to engage interactively with me, or learning what you need to will be difficult. Extend yourself and put forth effort into your understanding. Skill development is essential here to successfully completing this book and carrying superior trading skills with you, so see if you can answer these questions before looking down farther. It will also increase your powers of observation.

What is the general trend?

Now, look at Figure 8.2. Here we have a nice slope, no matter which general trajectory we use. The less aggressive lines still show healthy movement. The general trend is upward.

What do you observe about the size of the pullback noted at the top right of the chart? Once you've formulated an answer, look at Figure 8.3.

Figure 8.2 **General Trend Upward**

Figure 8.3 **Volatility and Pullback**

Figure 8.3 displays greater volatility, shown by long-range candles, engulfing each other often—meaning that price is in a whipsaw motion from candle to candle. There are also lower highs and lower lows. What can you say about the nature of the candle formations at the top right compared to the ones in the middle of the chart? From the same chart in Figure 8.3, we can see that the pullback wave here is much deeper than either pullbacks 1 or 2. The trending trade would be up, naturally—though as we progress and think about the way we look at stocks, this might not be as simple a statement as it appears.

What does this chart say about the next likely group of candles? Potential trend reversal will be created due to the strength of pullback.

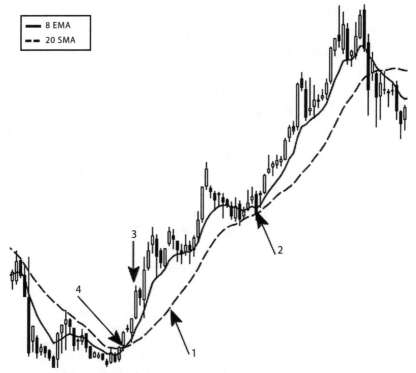

Figure 8.4 **The Moving-Average Trade**

Let's look at the moving-average trade in Figure 8.4.

When trading long, we can use several indicators, noted in Figure 8.4. Upward trends are confirmed when the crossover of the faster moving average *above* the slower moving average occurs (see arrow 4). Quite often this is used as an entry point at the confirmation candle above the crossover.

When we review a chart, notice where the candles are positioned. If most of the candles are printing above the moving averages, we are trending upward. Here's a rule of thumb: if you are in a long trade and the candles are printing above the averages, you're making money. The moment the candles cross below and begin to stay beneath the averages, the trade is losing ground. We also see that the moving-average lines are moving away from each other, seen at arrow 1, and closing in, at arrow 2. When averages are accelerating away from each other, the momentum is increasing in the direction of the move, and when they begin to drift closer, the strength of the move is diminishing. Flattening moving averages as shown at arrow 2 can signal a potential reversal, but until the candles begin to print beneath the averages and the moving averages change direction, we do not know for sure. Using moving averages to detect and confirm directional change is a common tool in trading, but it is lagging, meaning we get the information well after the fact.

Let's assume we come upon this chart at arrow 3. To make the most technically sound decision, when would we open this trade? We have two choices: wait to open the long trade at the bounce off the test of the 8 EMA or off the 20 SMA. How do we make the choice with these two options? Certainly, the better entry would be at the pullback to the 20 SMA, but will the chart make that move backward? Here's another rule of thumb: the sharper the acceleration, the less likely the pullback to the slower moving average. Due to the sharp move, we'll focus on the pullback to the 8. Our opportunity comes two candles later with the long-range candle. This implies patience. Wait for the formation or price to come to us. Don't make a habit of chasing trades.

Where would the relative stop be for this long? Draw a line where you think this support level should be. Notice we are not discussing actual numbers here but just looking at chart forms and decisions based on the forms alone.

Some possible stop levels that are aggressive and tight are shown in Figure 8.5.

Arrow 1 reveals a congestion level in the chart that could be used, and arrow 2 isolates our entry level and stop. When we have an ideal stop level like this, we can go lower by a few pennies. Our goal when trading is to enter as close to our stop as possible, minimizing our risk exposure.

What does a good long trade look like after we enter? Constant or increasing width between the moving averages and a continuing

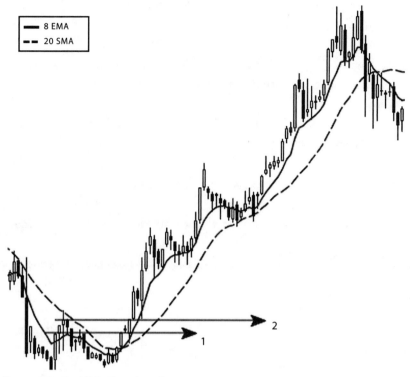

Figure 8.5 **Possible Stop Levels**

opportunity to continue to place higher stops as the trade continues. As the trade meanders north in solid fashion, our goal is to increase our size as our trade becomes stronger and also take the time to remove profits as events allow. We must pay attention to our trades. A lack of interest in stock movements, and our gains become fleeting and smaller than they could be. Keep on the lookout for any changes that might point to the trade being broken or slowing, and we'll consistently bank profits.

We entered at the test and rejection of the 8 EMA, but our opening position does not always have to be full size. The best practice I have discovered is to take a half-sized or quarter-sized entry position. Our goal is always to manage our exposure to risk. Carelessness in this area will lead to account depletions from which we might never recover. Where might we choose to take a full-sized position? Another way to ask this might be, where do you see the potential for this stock to have trouble? Or, at what level might we see a rejection of price? Take your pencil out and mark the level you believe that you would like to clear before adding to the position.

Take a look at Figure 8.6. Here's where that level is, at arrow 3. Can you answer why?

Here's a decision-making nuance that few books discuss. So we get to this level, but the behavior is less than decisive, so how are we to be definitive in our movement? Look at how many times the price hits that line in Figure 8.6. On that right side where we are to make an evaluation about adding to the size of our position, I count eight touches by candles. This is how we can tell a level is important. But what else can we look at to make the commitment to add? Where are

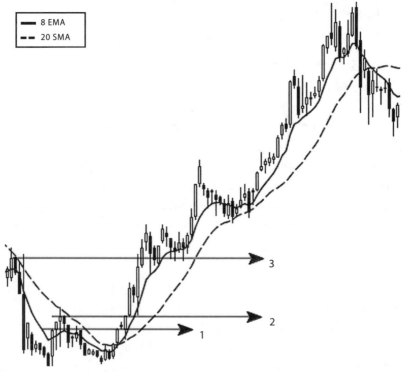

Figure 8.6 **Support Levels**

the candles ending? Above or below the 8 EMA? Above or below the level? The answers to these questions give us the directional choice. Just as long as the candles continue to close above the 8 EMA, we can add to this long and be patient in the hold. Let's use the pullback again into the 8 EMA *above* the new support level to add to the long in progress, above the level at arrow 3.

Though we have entered full sized, we are sitting in a trade that is now moving sideways. What clues can we see that might help us see where the stock might be continuing? The key observation is that the 8 EMA and the 20 SMA are still sloping upward. The closing in of the moving averages tell us things are slowing but not broken. This point is where many of us get shaken out of trades, without enough patience to wait it out when nothing in the chart formation is telling us to leave. Now, where do we place our focus? Take a look at Figure 8.7.

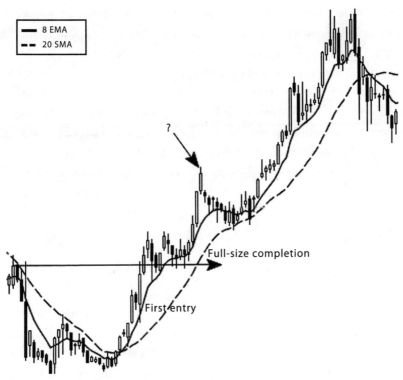

Figure 8.7 **First Entry and Full-Size Completion**

We should be pretty pleased with this trade. Where would we shift our stop up to preserve profits? To our first entry level, our breakeven spot. We need to constantly watch for reasonable places to set our new stops. They should not be arbitrary or based on what gains we are keen on keeping but instead on what makes sense in the natural rhythm of the stock.

Take a look at the huge spike at the question mark in Figure 8.7. This is a new decision area. Why? Huge parabolic expansions will retrace, and if we know this, we can position ourselves to benefit tremendously. How? Scaling.

Good scaling skills will catapult your account balance if trading high-momentum, high-volatility stocks. To scale this event properly, we need to address two things: parabolic expansion occurrence and the lagging of the 8 EMA, shown in Figure 8.8.

See that wide distance between the 8 EMA and the candle in Figure 8.8? That extension is like a rubber-band stretch. The two must draw closer to each other, and that means a price pullback. If it does not occur in the short order, it means a level of new acceleration is afoot. When that top candle spike begins its retrace off the high, it is time to capture profits. We can choose to remove one-half, or one-quarter—the choice is arbitrary. I customarily take one-half of the size off with the directed purpose of finding a new space to add back to the position, so that I may continue full size as the trade continues, so this is the strategy I recommend. Spikes like the one noted in our chart retrace as often as 80% of the time, so don't worry about chasing the trades. Have confidence that the price will come to you. Once the retreat begins, we estimate it must come in to test support. This support is usually defined by the last breakout level. See the area labeled "New support" in Figure 8.8. This area is where we will add full size to the position again.

Since our pullback into support, some sideways chatter appears again. Note that the price breaks the 8 EMA several times, but the secondary line of support we have at the 20 SMA holds steady as the price closes above, after every touch. Sideways action always brings

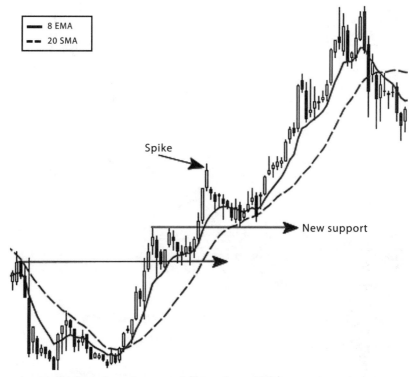

Figure 8.8 **Parabolic Expansion and Lagging 8 EMA**

moving averages closer together, but there are no crossovers, however, so our trend stays intact.

Another spike, shown in Figure 8.9, gives us the same opportunity to scale out. We have the same formations—distance expansion from the 8 EMA, parabolic expansion price movement—so we know we are in store for a retracement. Once we see the retreat from the top levels, we are safe to take profits and wait for the pullback into the 8 EMA to advance our position back to full size. We again move our stop up; this time possibly to the beginning of the large-range candle. Focus on the top of the chart in Figure 8.9—we'll see two more opportunities to move in the same scaling manner. For the sake of brevity here, I will ask you to walk through this on your own.

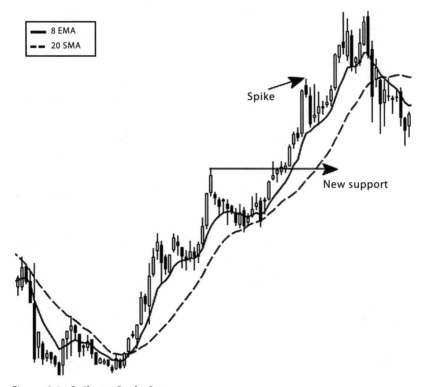

Figure 8.9 **Spike to Scale Out**

As our trade accelerates forward, Figure 8.10 shows where the newest stop should be placed. Why?

What do we see that shows this trade is broken and it is time to leave? Let's take a look at Figure 8.11, on page 116.

In Figure 8.11, arrows point to candles printing below the 8 EMA, the inflection, and reversal of the 8 EMA slope coupled with the moving-average crossover are a confirmation of momentum end, and reversal. We can leave at the break of new support, the crossover, or the print of candles below the 20 SMA. Broken support is what I like to use.

The separation of moving averages is always a good sign of momentum. When we have moving averages crossing over each other, it makes for very difficult trading.

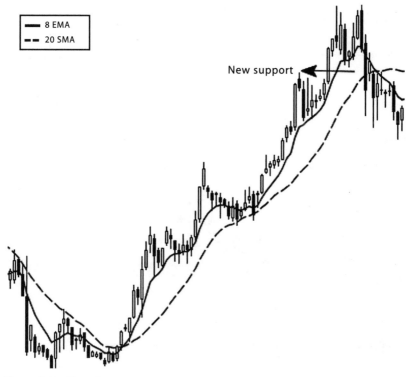

Figure 8.10 **New Support**

What do we notice about our trade walkthrough? We made observations of precise events that are detailed, organized, directed, and clearly defined—elements severely lacking in the trading plan of the average retail trader.

Bollinger Bands

We'll use the Bollinger bands here to walk us through the trade and provide the signals for us to move.

At first glance, what do we observe about the chart in Figure 8.12 as it relates to the Bollinger bands? See how much to the upper side of the band we see the candles? It is a sign of aggressive momentum. Using the bands here, where would we determine an

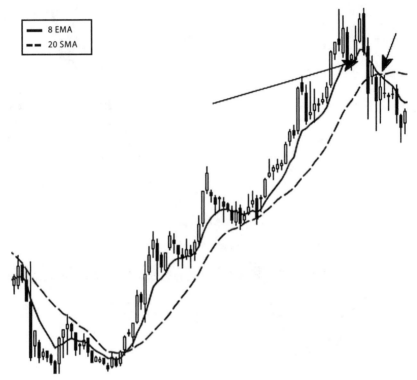

Figure 8.11 **Momentum End and Reversal**

entry to be? How about the confirmation candle above the mid-point line of the band? See the squeeze on the bands, or the "waisting," and the exaggerated expansion? This entry is a little more aggressive than our moving-average entry, and again, we'll go half size for our initial position. This "flanging" appearance is a clear sign in the bands that we have a breakout with a good sign of continuation. Though a pierce of the band generally means reversal, steep moves outward hint at the likelihood that the prices will hold closely to the band.

Managing stops in acceleration is always a little tricky, but look for where candles begin and end or congest to find the most likely stop. Reversal areas also make good stops for the trade. In Figure

Figure 8.12 **Aggressive Momentum**

8.13, we establish a stop at the base, where we see a lot of candles either beginning or ending right at this level.

The first time the stock begins to pull back from the upper band in sideways action is denoted by the hollow rectangle. Notice the base of the candles and look to the far left of the chart. Do you see where that level was observed in the past and now is holding in our present state? Where is the next likely stop? (We established that when we were observing the moving averages.)

In Figure 8.14, arrow 3 becomes the new stop as the stock continues to climb. At the breach of arrow 3, we can go to a full-size position. If the sideways action had resolved to the downside, our stop would have preserved profits, and our new entry would leave us

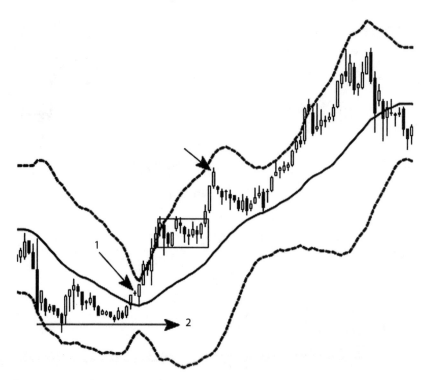

Figure 8.13 Behavior Near the Bollinger Bands

out flat with no losses. Instead, it broke to the upside. When a stock breaks out of a channel, the new stop should be moved to the bottom of the channel. If the channel is unusually large, price-wise, choose the midpoint as the stop. Arrow 4 points to expansion, and the information we have about candlesticks prepares us for the retracement of this move. It is not only the distance of the move that alerts us to possible pullback but the speed at which the movement occurs. So, to reiterate, when you see these spikes, take some of your position off and wait for the retrace to add. If you do not want to take such an active part in your portfolio management, just watch for signs that the trade is broken.

If you are keen on this kind of hands-on management, you'll be tired at the end of the day, for sure, but will carry home much more

Figure 8.14 **Next Stop and Expansion**

than your counterparts. If that puts some wind in your sails, let's continue. Take a look at the formation in Figure 8.15, occurring at the pullback from the spike and where it terminates.

We have a number of signals that suggest continuation upward is in the cards. The parallel lines define the bull flag, or a parallel movement downward in an uptrending chart, ending at the midline of the bands. This is an excellent area to add to our position so that we can continue upward with the size we are most comfortable to develop the trade. We can choose arrow 2, the test and bounce off the midline, or at arrow 3, the confirmation candle break outside the bull flag. At no time is our new stop level violated, arrow 1, so we hold nicely. As we follow our stop levels up, we still see acceleration signs with the steep slope in the upper band.

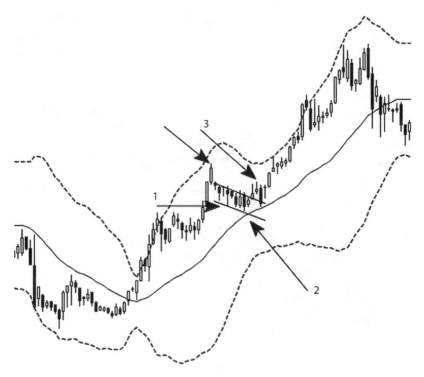

Figure 8.15 **Upward Continuation**

When can we establish the probability that the trade is broken? Arrow 2 in Figure 8.16 is the latest most natural stop because it is the breakout level just after the pullback from the long-range candle sitting just below the number 2. The candle formation noted by arrow 1 is a double top and is a key alert to the chance of reversal. Along with that, we see from the Bollinger bands that this retest of the high occurred away from the band. When new highs are created away from the band, the candles that follow will telegraph direction. Many times, that is a reversal formation, and we'll see lower prices.

The bands do not give us an alert to reversal in any other way here. So we are faced with trimming our position to half size at the pullback after the second spike, then closing the position out after

Figure 8.16 **Breakout Level**

the break of support level, arrow 2. Interestingly, this stop level coincides with the midpoint line of the bands, and this also signals the potential for change in direction and the cessation of momentum.

So what does the strength of the Bollinger bands reveal in this setup? Band expansion signals momentum breakout, and the location of the price prints do the same. Also, the relative higher highs occurring away from the bands give us a clue to a "peaking" event in the short term.

Fibonacci Retracements

Next, we'll take a look at this trade with the forward pricing tool of Fibonacci retracements. Fibs are not always best drawn from high to low but may indeed be best drawn from congestion levels of interest. We'll need a wide-angle view to look at the chart because, after all, the side of the chart we are analyzing hasn't actually occurred when we first draw the Fibonacci levels.

Key things to remember about Fibonaccis: they are only as good as they are drawn, and by themselves, they make vague trading tools. Here's what we can assume based on our chart formations:

1. We assume the trend is upward, which means that reversals to the upside seen in the chart will eventually fail.
2. After drawing the appropriate Fibs, we accept their reliability and trade them without questioning.

As the chapter on Fibonaccis shared with you, drawing them takes practice and "fitting." I'll assume you have worked on this and are becoming more comfortable with how they can deliver results for you. A Fib that fits poorly in the left side of the chart you "can" see will not fit well for the right side that has not developed. So, practice, practice, practice.

Note in Figure 8.17, our trigger points will be the breach of resistance that our relative congestion has created—remembering that failure of congestion regions will be followed by a retest of that level. Knowing this, we'll need to be patient. This statement will sound all too familiar to you as we progress.

Now see Figure 8.18, on page 124. Note the prior test of that 27.2% provides us with a resistance level to breach. Arrow 1 is the test, 2, the retest, and our entry point, long. To be most conservative, enter at the retest of breached levels, *unless* you have a great deal of volume or a breakaway formation. The break of the midline of the Bollinger bands and Fibonacci levels both show us the same entry long. Where should our stop be? The Fib level below is significantly beneath us, so we really don't like that one. Frankly, our entry is just about perfect according to Fib rules, and where our stop should be. This is ideal for us, as it limits our risk. Your stop beneath should be

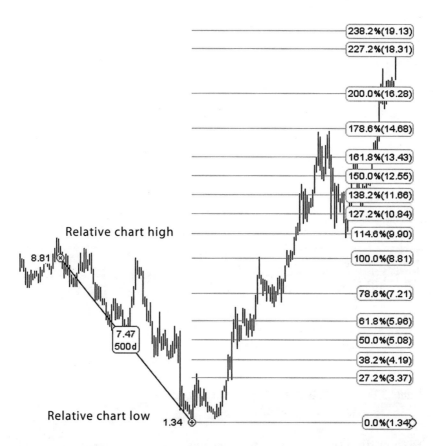

Figure 8.17 **Relative Chart High and Low**

tight—let's use .10 below. Honestly, a little arbitrary. Why choose .10? It gives us a little breathing room but gives us low risk. The *only* way we are able to set such a tight stop is because we have confidence in our drawn Fib levels.

Fibs consistently supply us with relevant levels of support and resistance. What can we use to measure momentum when we have no other technical? Indeed, it is support and resistance, so let's "eyeball" this chart in Figure 8.19 to see if we can identify these.

Based on the trading system we use, momentum is critical to keeping a trade in the green. Without moving averages or the bands

Figure 8.18 Test, Retest, and Entry Point

to show direction and trajectory, we need to catalog the measure and frequency of the failures to breach prior highs, and the continued losses of new lows. Conceptually, this should make sense since we are climbing up the rungs of support. We shouldn't fall through them if we have power in our move. The lack of the fallback in price confirms the strength of trend.

Take a look at both charts, Figure 8.18 and Figure 8.19, and notice how much confluence exists between support and resistance and the Fib levels. If we were going to be more granular, we would see that there is a Fib level at every level of support and resistance. Just like a tired climber will slip back to his last hold, tired moves in the charts will show these slips.

Let's begin the trade—long at 3.37—half size as we are concerned about the strength of the trade. Which level makes the most

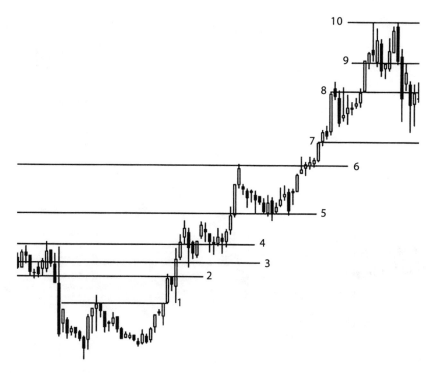

Figure 8.19 **Support and Resistance**

sense to go to full size? Take your pencil out and mark on the chart in Figure 8.20 where you would go to full size. Remember, we look to the left of the chart to estimate the potential problems in the future. Arrow 1 shows our addition point—again, notice the test-retest patterns. The more accustomed we become to seeing these formations, the less likely we are to have their appearance shake our confidence in our trade. Note the one candle that has a long wick testing below 5.08, *but* it does not close *below* the level. It's all about the candle close.

Let's look a little harder at this area that we chose to increase the size of our position. We know we need to take the trigger at the *confirmation* candle to be most conservative and have the highest level of reliability, but where would that put our entry if we use the rule of the confirmation candle completion versus the retest? If you

Figure 8.20 **Full Size**

were looking closely, you would see that these two rules will provide conflict about where to increase the size of this trade, but it could also have been the moment you chose to enter. So what do we do about the conflict?

Here is the general scenario. The test-retest "rule" is best applied at *important* levels of support and resistance; the confirmation candle "rule" is best used in other spaces like lesser levels and breaches or breaks of moving averages. The choice will ultimately be yours, and with time, you'll be able to pick which rule you should follow.

This is a fine distinction, and the only thing the choices do is provide you with a different level of risk opening the distance from your stop.

Look again at the chart in Figure 8.20 to determine where our new stop should be at the 5.08 entry. Shifting it up to the 38.2% level

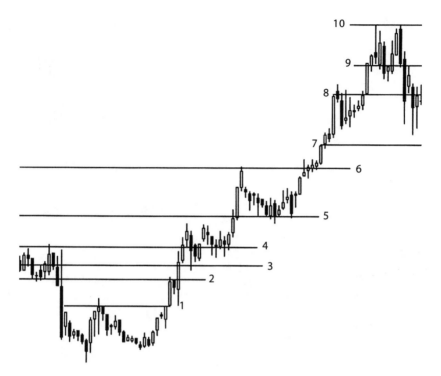

Figure 8.19 **Support and Resistance**

sense to go to full size? Take your pencil out and mark on the chart in Figure 8.20 where you would go to full size. Remember, we look to the left of the chart to estimate the potential problems in the future. Arrow 1 shows our addition point—again, notice the test-retest patterns. The more accustomed we become to seeing these formations, the less likely we are to have their appearance shake our confidence in our trade. Note the one candle that has a long wick testing below 5.08, *but* it does not close *below* the level. It's all about the candle close.

Let's look a little harder at this area that we chose to increase the size of our position. We know we need to take the trigger at the *confirmation* candle to be most conservative and have the highest level of reliability, but where would that put our entry if we use the rule of the confirmation candle completion versus the retest? If you

178.6%(14.68)
161.8%(13.43)
150.0%(12.55)
138.2%(11.66)
127.2%(10.84)
114.6%(9.90)
100.0%(8.81)
78.6%(7.21)
61.8%(5.96)
50.0%(5.08)
38.2%(4.19)
27.2%(3.37)
1.34
0.0%(1.34)

Figure 8.20 Full Size

were looking closely, you would see that these two rules will provide conflict about where to increase the size of this trade, but it could also have been the moment you chose to enter. So what do we do about the conflict?

Here is the general scenario. The test-retest "rule" is best applied at *important* levels of support and resistance; the confirmation candle "rule" is best used in other spaces like lesser levels and breaches or breaks of moving averages. The choice will ultimately be yours, and with time, you'll be able to pick which rule you should follow.

This is a fine distinction, and the only thing the choices do is provide you with a different level of risk opening the distance from your stop.

Look again at the chart in Figure 8.20 to determine where our new stop should be at the 5.08 entry. Shifting it up to the 38.2% level of 4.19 is most acceptable. Now look at the behavior at the golden ratio of 61.8% and 5.96. It's choppy; it breaks the plane but fails to confirm once, then a pullback to the 50% and a bounce back into 61.8%, and again a pullback.

Keep looking at Figure 8.20. What's different about the second pullback? Buyers are propping up the price *above* the 50% level now. This should telegraph that the next tests should press higher. And they do, but still fail. As we keep looking at this trade and get anxious, what should we do according to the Fib rules? Are we violating support levels? No. That means strength is still there. We get itchy to leave trades in spots like this, and we should not.

Our reward? See the chart in Figure 8.21 as the breakout levels continue through the 78.6% and the 100% retracement levels. Where should we shift the stop after the breach of 7.21?

Figure 8.21 **Breakout and Continuation**

Naturally, 61.8 and 5.96 makes sense. The 100% Fib level is the
focal point in the chart, as is 200% and 300%, and reversal there
is almost a given. If we are managing our trade aggressively, we
will *plan* to remove half of our position at the *test* of this level.
We do not wait for confirmation candles here, as we assume a
rejection will occur. This is true more than 85% of the time in
my experience.

Now look at the next frame of observations in Figure 8.22.

The retracement occurs on cue. It is a little deep but does not
come into our stop. What do we do when we feel concern about the
depth of a pullback like this one? To stop emotional and impulsive
moves, we need to ask ourselves something simple: is the stock trade
broken? How do we know? Notice the left side of arrow 1? As this
retracement starts and continues, look to the left to see if we're going
to slip off that "rung," the prior old resistance and new support. As

Figure 8.22 **Retracement**

long as we hold relative support, our trade is intact, so all we need is patience. We can add at the recapture of the 78.6% level.

How do we define that recapture? Because of the congestion formation, we need to wait for the confirmation candle, as 78.6% is one of the *lesser* levels. We can add to the trade at this stage. When we reclaim 8.81 and the 100% level, we can shift the stop to the 7.21 region, and add again to the position if we are so inclined.

We are observing something simple that we hear about all the time—let your winners run. But that takes what? Yes! You're getting it—patience. Learn to wait things out if all seems well.

When the price rockets into that 38.2%, it is time to take more profits. Look at Figure 8.23.

We should go to half our size again with this breach formation into 11.66, shown with arrow 3. At the pullback and bounce off the prior level, we can add once more at the confirmation candle, and

Figure 8.23 **Breach Formation**

again at arrow 4, raising our stop to the next Fib level once it clears the one just above it. Kinda like lather, rinse, repeat—we are not fighting the currents of the moves but taking advantage of them. Our new stop is around 12.45 due to the wicks seen nearby that broke the level. Notice that if we do this at the second top to the right of arrow 4, we will not be able to add to the position because there is no bounce above our 12.55 or 150% level like there was the first time. The failure should provide the urge to take more profits, and we should close the position once the stop is breached.

Bringing Them All Together

Now, with all our pieces together, let's walk through the decision-making process involving all the technicals together. This is what our charts will look like (Figure 8.24), but I would very much rec-

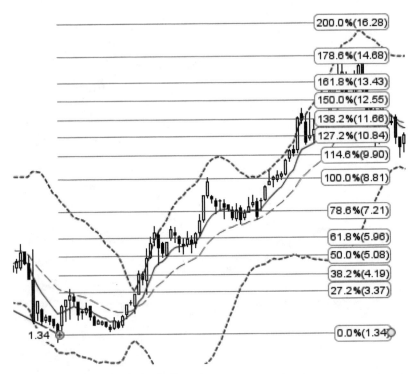

Figure 8.24 **All the Technicals Together**

ommend that when you consider a chart for the first time, look at it in layers as we just did.

Step through the indicators with me as they occur—see how they follow through and create our system of measured stops as we walk through the trade. The key indicators are numbered in Figure 8.25.

Label 1 represents where we picked up the chart for review. We have several choices for entry: the moving-average crossover at 2, the confirmation candle of the break above the 20 SMA at 3, or the breach of prior resistance of the 3.37 price level first isolated at 1. The most conservative is the breach of 3.37, as this comes after a series of other events pointing to the power of the breach. Label 4 identifies the breakout level above the golden ratio reflection of 38.2% as well as the expanding bands. Label 5 shows us to the confluence of both the 61.8% and the Bollinger band breach and

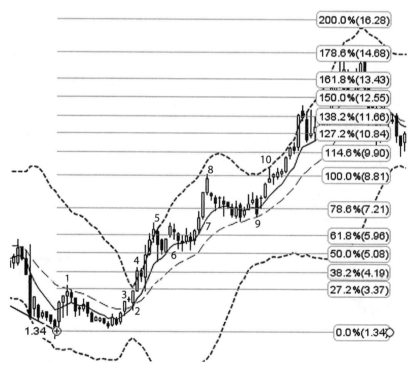

Figure 8.25 **Stepping Through the Indicators**

introductory pullback into the 50% level for the test of new support at 6. Recovery comes at recapture of 61.8% and the bounce off the 8 EMA at 7, with the new expansion and the first test of the 100% level (that we expect to fail) at 8—noticing all the while that price continues to print nicely above the 8 EMA, confirming our confidence in the move is well placed. Label 9 shows a pullback and bounce into Fib levels that allows us to increase our size, and finally the retest and breach of the 100% level happens at 10.

Let's advance the chart in Figure 8.26 to walk through the climb forward.

Label 11 presents a breach of the golden ratio reflection at 138.2% and a breach outside the Bollinger band. Like clockwork, these combined formations allow for adding at the pullback seen at

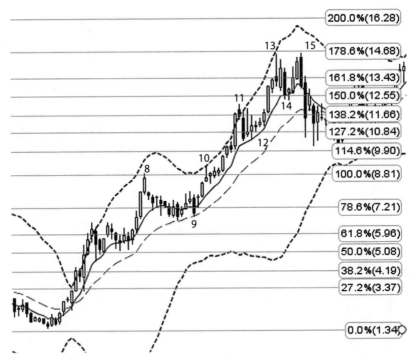

Figure 8.26 **The Climb Forward**

12 after the removal of gains at the observance of that prior breach. The topping tail at 13 should cause us to clear more gains and the pullback to the standard 150% at 14 again with the bounce off the 8 EMA, where we can add more as we estimate a 200% might be in the works. The failure of the 150% level combined with the loss of the 8 EMA should cycle us out of the trade.

CONCLUSION

I'd like to present this simplistically once more just by directive at each number in the trade. We'll assume 1,000 shares is our full size. Take a look again at Figures 8.25 and 8.26.

1.   Chart identification.
2./3.   Observances 1 and 2 and entry 500 shares at 3.37; stop set just below 2.
4.   Add 500 shares at 4.19 breach.
5.   Remove 500 shares at 5.96 test.
6.   Add 500 shares at 5.08.
7.   Raise stop to 5.08.
8.   Remove 500 shares at 8.81 test.
9.   Add 500 shares at 7.21 breach.
10.   Raise stop to 7.21.
11.   Remove 500 shares at 11.66.
12.   Add 500 shares at 10.84 hold and raise stop to 9.90.
13.   Remove 500 shares at rollover near 14.68.
14.   Add 500 shares at 12.55 and raise stop to 11.66.
15.   Remove 500 shares at rollover from 14.68 and raise stop to 12.55.

Note action step 15: This identifies the new stop loss. A break of this price, 12.55, is the signal to exit the trade.

Of course, everything is simple when we walk through it after the fact. It is in the middle of the day when we are observing candlestick action that we make hasty and impulsive decisions that diminish our gains. Walk through this again and see that it all makes sense. Our minds have a tendency to glaze over details—which is why eyewitness accounts are statistically some of the worst things to count on. The more we focus on the details, the easier decision making will become.

CHAPTER 9

Your Trading Journal

"Never walk away from failure. On the contrary, study it
carefully and imaginatively for its hidden assets."

—MICHAEL KORDA

I'd like to take a moment here to break from our more technical discussion and detail an aspect of trading that I have alluded to in the previous chapters of this book: the trading journal. Though paramount to success, creating and using a trading journal daily seems to be on those "I'll eventually get around to that" lists we make. My husband calls such procrastination the "BenGunna syndrome," as in, "I've bengunna do that" (I think the reference is to someone he knew in the military). Sometimes, I'm Chief BenGunna, but I really don't want to be: as soon as I think of myself like that, I pretty much snap out of it.

I'm not quite sure why so many of us resist writing and keeping trading journals, but I do know why I was a BenGunna. I resisted the urge early on because it seemed like a lot of work that would actually interrupt my trading, then I resisted because I did not know what to write down, then because I felt a bit lazy, and then because the last thing I wanted to do was review horrifying trades to remind me about how bad I was. (I mean, seriously, who wants to scour over terrible mistakes? Um, not me.) There are probably more reasons, but those are the ones I remember repeating to myself.

Maybe I resisted because I realized that I wasn't really figuring out what the market was all about; maybe it was the constant missteps, repeating mistakes that were very familiar; maybe it was the feeling I was like a hamster running on a treadmill going twice my speed that made me come to the realization that what I had been doing had given me what I had gotten, and since I didn't like the state I was in, writing a trading journal (as well as a lot of other changes) started looking *really good* to me.

Fact: if we do not carefully review our trades, why our trades were good or went bad escapes us. We might think we know, but if we have not completed forensic analysis, we will miss the finer points and movements in the market. Think of the trading journal as our notebook during the class lecture; we jot down thoughts and observances of important pieces, formations, ideas, and other mechanics. Only after class do we get the chance to really absorb the material. Consider the market. We get quizzed every day on the information we learned the day before or new information we have never seen.

If we think about things a little more like that, we most certainly will look at a journal in a different light. Careful documentation and review of the trading journal lays the foundation for a mistake-free day, and since my journal writing began, I have had many of these. The trading journal catapults the trader to the consistent execution of perfect trades. Notice, I am not saying all the trades were green on all those days, but that only the execution of the system was flawless. Nothing works 100% of the time in the market—*nothing*. If it did, a great number of us skilled in market pattern study would have already purchased islands in French Polynesia, or wherever, and hired a full staff to tend to us as we lived in very large glass-bottomed bungalows out in the sea (fill in your own ideal situation above).

MY EARLY YEARS

Here's an excerpt from my own trading journal:

> Tried to pay attention to the way the market moved in the morning. I still don't know why whips throw me out of so many trades. Didn't see the trigger to enter on some trades but watched others go by. I'm scared to death. Fearful to make decisions, waiting too long, entering too late, exiting too early. Yesterday, I finally got out of the APA trade—short call spread that was deep in the money, was just waiting for it to get back green, and it kept going more red every day, so I capitulated and bought them back at 60% loss, only to see the stock skyrocket today. I cannot remember the last time I lost my temper so dreadfully. I smashed my mouse on the floor—and screamed at the top of my lungs in rage. The market makes me so crazy, but the thought of giving up does not remotely exist. Internal dialogue very negative, horrific. I'd never speak to another human the way I find myself doing to myself—and often for failed trades. Gotta stop that. I'm just so tired of wondering what the heck I'm doing and wondering if I will ever get a friggin' clue. I work so hard preparing for the day, and it feels like it's all for nothing. It's like I'm looking at everything and seeing nothing at all. That's the part that makes me cry at the end of the day. I get the feeling there is so much I don't know, and it feels very lonely—I feel alone.

When I decided to write this book, I wondered which experiences would be best suited to make for a greater understanding, and though I had some great examples from the many people I've worked with as a coach and mentor, I decided to painfully open some of my own journals. Viewing evidence of an incredible number of trading mistakes, I recalled not having a real trading system even though I thought I did at the time. I didn't really troubleshoot train wreck trades that needed it, and I was incompetent at managing risk. I feel that exposing this aspect of my trading life, opening the inside of the struggle to trade, would be worth more to the trader who wants to see part of the emotional journey to competence. It will forever be painful to remember, but the lessons were priceless in the building of mental strength and eventual expertise.

Here's what I learned along the way—if you don't believe you can do it, you won't. Trading for a living takes iron will, and you'll see me write that often in this book. This point needs to be somehow ingrained into our psyches, or we will crumble. For the person who is swing trading for income, the emotions are the same. We day traders just feel it more times a day than they do.

As I look through my early journals, I notice a great many things that I could not have seen while I was making the journal entries. I particularly notice I am looking at the surface of the market. Imagine this: Let's say the market is one of those miniature cities we see built on the boardroom tables of any James Bond film (seems evil geniuses have a fetish for model structures). Now looking down at the miniature complex, envision a wrap of tight cellophane over the market. The cellophane reflects in some places and makes it difficult for you to see through. It reflects you, some of your surroundings, or nothing at all. This is how the newer or inexperienced trader looks at the market. There is an invisible layer that hides market truths from us, and we base our decisions on surface knowledge. The skill comes with your ability to unwrap and reveal your little corner of the market.

I also noticed that I seemed to be reviewing dozens and dozens of stocks and doing hours and hours of work, but a funny thing would happen on the way back to my desk the next morning: I'd become snow-blind at the opening bell, seized by inaction.

I think a common belief among newer traders is that the more they study, the easier it will be to get the best trade. Indeed, I find the reverse to be true. If you focus on only a few stocks, you will make better trades, provided you have a real system in place. Let go of the idea that you are there to hit the home run, to find the stock that moves 70% in one day. It will make you feel like you are missing out on everything, and that does nothing but frustrate you, and frustration makes for poor trading. Try picking just a few stocks and learning them well. If you intend on being a momentum trader, find stocks that move, ones with high betas.

The term *high beta* means that a stock moves at a faster rate than the broad market. That is, if the broad market moves one point, and your stock moves three points for every one point the market moves, it is a high-beta stock. Learn what they trade like—ask yourself if the stock has a particular rhythm, a price level it seems to be gravitating around, any releases, earnings, conference calls. Understanding just a handful, 10 or 20 names, will give you command of the area that you have chosen to trade.

We feel so much is out of our control when we are trading with insufficient knowledge. When we make our universe a bit smaller, we gain more control over what we are choosing to trade, choosing with whom we dance. One of the turning moments in my trading career came when I realized I did not have to scan the vast amounts of information out there for me to find that one morsel of information that would make a difference in the day. So much pressure slipped away.

If you have a good trading system and patience to wait for the setups, all you'll ever need is a few stocks to make a living. Yes, you'll see the winsome wish of catching that blazer all over Twitter, but successful, consistent trading comes from taking gains, a little at a time, every day. And, not to worry, the big trades will find their way to you if you are working in the right baskets.

I refer to my trading journal often. I notice that I never really stop getting angry with myself for making stupid trades, and I seem to always have some large element of emotion appearing on the pages. However, nowadays, I immediately review the trade, looking at the candles and possible telltale formations that could have stopped me from entering the trade. Sometimes, it is still the right thing to do, and sometimes I will just miss the most simple things. Every day is a battle to pay attention to the right signals.

FROM SUCCESS TO DEFEAT

Here's another excerpt from my own journal:

> Yesterday, I did soooo well. Everything I touched seemed to work. [The prior day's entry ended with, "I'm so excited, I think I really have it. I can't wait for tomorrow."] But today, today was like so many others, filled with what seemed like brand-new mistakes and very familiar and often repeated ones. Trading is like poker, you know, anyone with money can step up to the table, but not just anyone can leave with more than they came with. Defeat snatched from the jaws of victory, I like to say. After two days of real success to have today end in crushing defeat, I am more dismayed than I would be having two bad days in a row. At least I expect two bad days in a row.
>
> Then there's the garbage floating around myself about being stupid and a moron for making the mistakes I made today. I sit here dreaming of electroconvulsive shock therapy—I would have to think then, and I'm sure I wouldn't feel this anvil on my chest. If I try to think about what I did wrong, I can see that I either sold at the very bottom or went long at the very top. Why in the world did I do that? When I hesitate, the trades run without me; when I jump in quickly, the trades go against me. I'm so uncertain, day after day, trade after trade—nothing in sight but a sea of red, but I can't stand the thought of quitting because I've convinced myself there is nothing else for me to do. That this is it and nothing else. I'm feeling trapped and already dreading tomorrow. How ridiculous is that?
>
> I did finally put my system on silent today because when I hear the chime of an executed order, I start to feel sick to my stomach. I'm a Pavlovian dog. The execution time is for me to throw my lunch up to confirm I did something wrong. Only a matter of time before the proof of that shows

up with another red trade. I stopped eating during the day. I feel nauseous when I am in front of the desk. When am I ever going to get this? I guess I need to really sit and pore over my trades, but finally the thought of looking over the mistakes makes me feel like stepping in front of a speeding transit bus. Today, I got so scared after 11 A.M. that I tore all my fingernails off and left them in piles on a corner of my desk. Trading might be making me insane.

You know, as I sifted through the hundreds of journal pages over the years, I clearly remember that journal entry. It seems somewhat light-hearted as I reread it, but I remember that I did walk through my trades after that. I sat for hours, hands raking through my hair, and finally face in hands, weeping over my losses, wanting to be so much, and feeling like I was ending up as so little.

Before I decided to include this entry in this book, I ran my fingers over the tear-stained pages, and the flood of emotion washed right over me like it was yesterday. New tears splashed right on those old ones, and as I pushed the journal aside remembering the dark days, a new pool of them collected beneath my chin. I wondered why I was crying quite so hard, thumbing through this section of entries, and I could feel that core emotion from the past of raw desire and hopelessness—knowing that there was no one I could turn to for answers, no one to share knowledge with me, and no one to confess demoralizing defeat to.

I remember beginning to read a lot more technical trading books about that time, some of them quite good, and some of them barely good enough for kindling, but I was picking up mechanics. When I reviewed this particular day's trades for the second time, I had not done so for several months. I was glad I had always kept good notes (even though I would not review them until much later—seems I had to get the taste of general disgust with my performance out of my mouth), so I found the time frames on my trading platform and discovered a few things about my trading that were not remotely evident to me at the time I wrote the entries:

- I had no planned exit.
- I had no patience for the trade to develop (most likely because I had no confidence in my ability to read the trade correctly).
- I could not seem to find written down any rationale for my entering the trades.
- Most important, I was not assessing my risk and risk exposure at any time. I also did not seem to stop trading after a string of dreadful trades.

This last realization was a momentous event in my trading career. It was insane how much risk I took. That began the pivotal turn in my career.

I have dozens of journals, some of which I use for research and aftermarket study, and some for my daily trades and musings. The months of journal writings chronicling major defeat were gut-wrenchingly emotional, ramblings of a trader at her wits' end, but every day I just kept coming back. About every six weeks, I'd break them out and read over the past trades, and though the queasy feeling stayed reading many of them, it was invaluable—like a road map in the dark and a chance to review actions with a mind no longer clouded by the emotions of that day. Reading my old trades and talking them *out loud* was critical to my advancement as a trader.

Trading as a retail trader is a painful journey. I sometimes wonder what it would be like to have had some knowledge of the market—someone who had started with a trading house then moved out on my own. But the more I think about the unique way I trade, I'm not so sure that my style would have developed with all those other influences.

ALRIGHT, ALREADY: HOW DO I DO IT?

Get a notebook, or create and name a Microsoft Word, OneNote, or Excel file on one of those screens and keep it open all day to note critical events about your trades. For me, halfway to 90, I'm a little old-school and enjoy putting my favorite pen to paper to record these things. When I first started, I put simple things down like what economic releases were coming that day and paid particular attention to the first part of the months' releases. Then I would just record my entries and exits, and after the day was done, I would try to write about the emotion bubbling up in me over the day. Sometimes this was cathartic, sometimes not; but by rereading these entries, I began to understand more about myself and my impulse "triggers."

As I became more comfortable with the writing element, I recorded the aftermarket and premarket range of the e-minis, or ES_F as the symbol is most commonly seen. Why? Range is an important clue to what may lie ahead for us in the day. So many people just look at the open market for U.S. trading—I do not. I believe that everything that happens in the charts is worth some review as clues appear out of nowhere on occasion. Simply observing overnight movement and comparing it to the day's range over and over again, I was able to discover this fact, but without my journal, I would probably never have found it.

Be Pragmatic

At the time, I also used my journal for researching stocks and logging events that might move a sector or actually revealed a move in a sector of interest. I began researching hundreds of stocks. I kept 20-hour days for many months. I would chose 30 to look at and write down reams of data. But when the bell rang, I was chasing trades and following Twitter. Ridiculous. I chronicled that as well and realized that less is more. We research so many stocks because we are so afraid of missing the big run somewhere. News flash—we're always going to miss some big run somewhere, so how about just scanning for the top three runners and work with them?

How can we find runners? There are so many market screeners out there—AlphaScanner (http://www.alphscanner.com), Brian Shannon's excellent market tool, for one, and FinViz (http://www.finviz.com) for another—that can identify movers quickly to analyze. Do a search on stocks 10% or less from their current highs to find momentum. Less is more in this business. And here we were thinking the more we knew the better off we were. Who knew. As I mentioned in the section on filtering the noise in Chapter 1, if what we pack in to our study to exhaustion does not produce more consistent winning trades, we may as well be watching reality television or doing some other mindless brain pollution. Become very pragmatic in the trading journal. If it doesn't make for better trading or better gains, kick it to the curb.

When I finally started refining what I looked at (see the excerpts of my entries) and understanding that there was such a thing as too much homework, the sections of research in my journal became much smaller, and a more refined focus allowed me to find what I deemed were good entry points. I began to ask myself these questions before every trade:

- Why am I taking this trade?
- Where do I anticipate this stock moving?
- What do I expect to gain from the trade?

I found out that I was taking trades while being completely unable to even answer these basic questions. I also realized that my decision-making process was "soft" and lacked any kind of confirmation event. Though I had researched a core group and was keeping my eyes on those, I was still trading impulsively, both in and out, and filled with emotions of fear and angst. It was arduous, and once I began to record these emotions next to my trades, it was like a thunderbolt to me. I had exposed the way I was trading to myself. I could not see the mistakes until after the fact, until after I began to write the same things day after day and was always asking why. What I was using to trade was unable to give me the confidence I was working in a stock that was not going to break down on me. And that got me to work on developing something I could rely on.

Good trading systems are almost like your favorite most comfortable chair. What?! It's coming. Though when we are younger we do this much more, I'd like you to imagine just jumping into the chair to relax. Just throw yourself on there. It's a good chair, and it supports you well, and you know it is going to be an enjoyable experience. It doesn't give out on you, so you can dive into it with confidence. Now let's say that routinely, one out of every five times and sometimes at random, when you jump into that chair, it collapses on you, and the frame hits you squarely in the head, leaving you with a large, very painful knot as a souvenir. Are you going to dive into that chair with abandon now? Unless you've been hit in the head one too many times already, you are going to answer in the negative. How are you going to sit in the chair? If your response is, "Sit in it? Are you crazy? I'm getting rid of that chair," though probably the smartest thing to do, it won't fit our analogy, so I beg you to play along. Are you going to look for obvious signs of robustness, or security? Are you going to look for flaws that you might work on so it does not break down like that? And when you do enter, you'll be ginger getting in there, won't you? More careful to feel the sides or seat for any kind of failure. This only makes sense.

However, trading and sensibility often seem to be far away from each other, and the most simple things feel dangerous and complex. See, trading systems are like the chair, and how you get in is the way you enter trades. Remarkably, my journal writing illuminated that I had a chair that broke down 50% of the time. I would get smacked in the head, crawl out of the chair, bumped and bruised—and then do it all over again without looking for what might be wrong with the chair. This book is about making that chair rock solid but, at the same time, making sure that we are still always cautious on approach.

Sample Journal

For those of us struggling with structure, let's see how a simple journal might look. As a side note, our trading platforms should be able to show us the high and low of aftermarket activity, and websites like Econoday (http://econoday.com) will give a calendar breakdown of events.

Date: Wednesday, Jan. 12

Premarket Movement: ES_F range 5 points wide from high to low. Asia market open spike; Euro market open—no change.

Economic Releases and Times of Release: Import/export prices 8:30 A.M.; petroleum report 10:30 A.M.

Top Five Stocks to Watch
- AAPL: looking for a break out of the channel; alert set
- OIH: moving average resistance, Fib level above; alert set
- BAC: unusual volume, watching for confirmation candle of breakout; need to set alert
- BIDU: moving on news, watching for continuation; alert set
- CMG: surprising breakdown yesterday; looking for recovery

Market Events and Trends
- Bought OIH at 138.12 (10:23 A.M.), out all at 136.77 (10:35); forgot about petroleum report—pay attention
- Bought AAPL at 340.35 (11:45 A.M.); out ½ at 342.20 (12:15 P.M.); out rest at 340.70 (1:25 P.M.); stock still running; left too early (try to find out why)

Aftermarket Review
Market (ES_F) kept in the opening range most of the day. Forgot about the release and traded in front of it—loss. OIH recovered later—didn't get back in, too scared. Not even sure why I took that OIH trade; it didn't even feel right, but I did it anyway. Poor decision-making process there. Good entry in AAPL but out too early in trade because I was nervous about losing profits. Stop too tight.

It's as simple as that. Add more, but any less is not going to be as beneficial to fine-tuning ability and acumen.

CONCLUSION

Once a rhythm is established, it is much easier to maintain a journal than originally assumed. Make journal keeping a habit. Failing to have some kind of journaling process that opens the chance for careful review of trades is as good as sealing failure as our fate.

Until we firmly decide what we are doing is incorrect, we'll fall back into old habits and old mistakes and muddle them together with new skills and techniques and still end up making bad trades. Using this trading system and its associated strategies requires a bit of mental "scrubbing" and a release of the "well, I've always done it that way" thoughts. For some of us that will be a battle royale.

If you don't have a trading journal or do not chronicle your trades, you will do yourself a great disservice and postpone your consistent successful days further back. Are you pleased with the level of skill you have? If you are, you probably shouldn't be. If you don't work every day at being better than the day before, even in some small way, you'll wake up, and the market will have passed you by. Your skills will wane, and you'll eventually become ineffective. If you desire a high level of skill, it means you must do something different, something more, something more difficult. Being diligent about a trading journal, writing what you think, why you made the trade, and what/when you executed the trade, will prove itself as one of the best things you ever did to increase your trading skill; it was for me. Change is simple if we just realize that change is nothing more than a choice.

CHAPTER 10

From Simple to Complex: Short Trade

"Nothing in this world can take the place of persistence. Talent will not; nothing is more common than unsuccessful people with talent. Genius will not; unrewarded genius is almost a proverb. Education will not; the world is full of educated derelicts. Persistence and determination alone are omnipotent. The slogan 'press on' has solved and always will solve the problems of the human race."

—CALVIN COOLIDGE

Most of us are very familiar with long trades—we'll buy at a price that we expect the stock will rise from, only to sell them later at a greater price. On the other hand, short trades are often difficult for the retail trader. However, the process of selling short or borrowing shares you do not have in order to sell them, so that you may buy them back at a cheaper price than you sold them, is essentially the reversal of the movements of a long trade. Short trades are extremely lucrative, and it is very often the case that the short trade will leave you in a profitable state far more quickly than the long trade will—provided that you have chosen the correct side of the trade. I like selling short because it allows me to capture profit quickly and stay in the market a shorter period of time.

THE SHORT-TRADE WALKTHROUGH

Though the rules remain the same for short and long trades, the decisions are inverted, so it makes sense to walk through the short trade in just as detailed measure as the long one. Again, we will begin with the moving averages and general trends. My language and action outline will be very similar to the long trade because I want to emphasize the need for a uniform approach to trades and trading. Let's take a look at the chart we'll be trading this time. We'll need a wide angle to begin (see Figure 10.1).

Because we've just done a walkthrough in Chapter 8, I've made the chart analysis a little tougher here. Using the white space in Figure 10.1, again jot down answers to the following questions:

1. What is the general trend?
2. Is this a weak or strong stock, and why?
3. What direction would the trending trade be?
4. What does this chart say about the next likely group of candles?

Engage here so that you might learn actively. If you wait for me to tell you the answers every time, you will not be thinking or using both inductive and deductive logic—and you need these skills to advance.

What is the general trend, as shown in Figure 10.2, on page 152?

Though the top of the chart shows low to high, the body of the chart is sideways, and the bottom of the chart says up. Conflicting signals. Let's leave the answer to that question as undetermined. It is clear it is in flux.

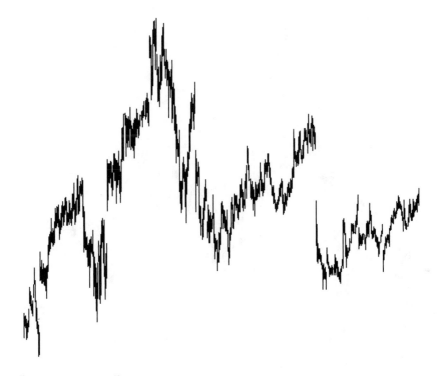

Figure 10.1 **Base Chart**

Is this a weak or strong stock? Take a look at Figure 10.3. Though the trend seems undetermined, the large gap in the middle of the chart displays weakness. It is a picture of the typical break-away gap to the downside—usually news-based or earnings-release information.

The last half of the chart in Figure 10.3 looks like the stock is bouncing, but our rules about gaps say that if the stock is unable to recapture the broken levels at the test, there is more downside continuation.

What direction would the trending trade be? This is difficult, and to answer, we must view the chart as painting a picture. The numbers on the chart in Figure 10.4, on page 154, represent lower lows and lower highs—a negative trend. The gap displays funda-mental weakness. The chart also shows that sellers are present at the

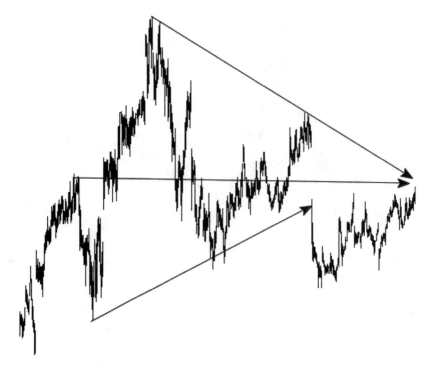

Figure 10.2 **In Flux**

entry to the gap. All negative, but if that is the case, what does the arrow running along the newest wave in the chart identify?

The arrow is showing a corrective wave, and corrective waves provide the setups for the trending trade. Therefore, we are waiting on a break in the formation back to the downside in order to begin the trade. Many of us would have chosen to go long here on the chance there was a recovery, but that would be incorrect. Whether we realize it or not, our minds are geared to anticipate the incorrect forward motion in the chart. What does this chart say about the next likely group of candles? We are looking for a break in the upside formation. What might we want to see to trigger the short trade?

In Figure 10.5, on page 155, the support level is noted by arrow 1. This type of price hold is sometimes called *congested support* due to the choppy action around the price level. There are few

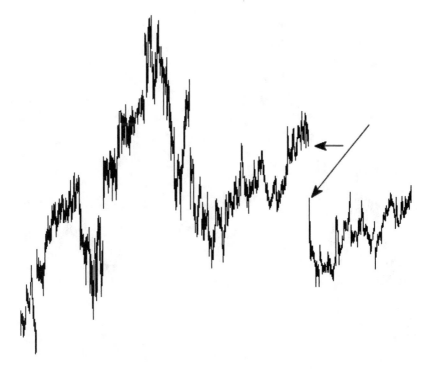

Figure 10.3 **Weak Formation**

moments where clear rejection or bounce support holds. Were you
able to see this clearly? The aggressive short would be at the direct
gap-fill region, arrow 2, but we see that it broke that already, and so
the odd chance exists that the stock will reverse and hold the new
uptrend. Let's telescope in and open up the right side of the chart to
begin the after-the-fact walkthrough of this short trade. Arrow 3 in
Figure 10.5 shows where we picked up this chart.

Now we will step through the moving-average trade in Figure
10.6, on page 156. Look at the top left of this chart. Point 1 is where
we caught sight of this chart and chose the level to break in order to
go short. In hindsight, was this the appropriate level for the trigger?
Before you read forward, consider what I might be driving you to
observe. I'll ask you this in another way. If a stock breaks a level to
the downside, and we take the trade, what do we do if it recaptures

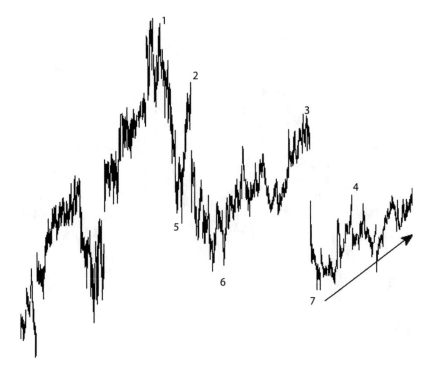

Figure 10.4 **Corrective Wave**

the broken level? The answer: we would get stopped out. *Please* don't lollygag in trades that do this. Simply get out and *wait* for the right setup once more.

For the sake of illustration, let's assume we took this trade at the break of the level in order to observe a few things. As with all entry positions, we chose a quarter-size or half-size position. Consider the region in Figure 10.7, on page 156, identified by arrow 1. Here observe a negative moving-average crossover that confirmed a decision to go short, then just a few candles later, a positive moving-average cross-over, arrow 2, which invalidated our directional slant. By the time we got above the crossover, we had broken above to recapture the price level we initially lost in the region of the first moving-average crossover. Once a stock regains a price in this manner, it is show-

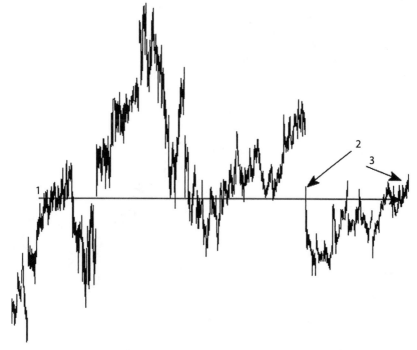

Figure 10.5 **Congested Support**

ing strength, and short positions should be cautiously observed. This
should have been a clear exit for us. Often, we'll just gaze and wait to
see what happens. Granted, if we had followed our signals, we'd be
just fine at this point—out of the trade, but what if it had not stopped
moving up? Where would you have gotten out of the trade? At the
next support/resistance level up? And how much more red would the
trade be by then?

The trick is to get out when things look bad and *wait* (that word
again) for the setup to trigger once more. Remember, if a setup does
not work the first time, it does not mean it won't work the next time.
That is another dreadful habit we have trading. If a trade goes against
us and we have to get out, we'll throw that stock and setup to the side
when what we should be doing is waiting for the next opportunity.

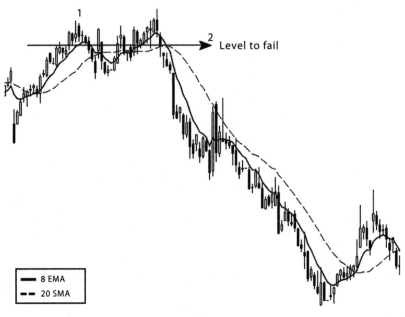

Figure 10.6 **The Moving-Average Trade**

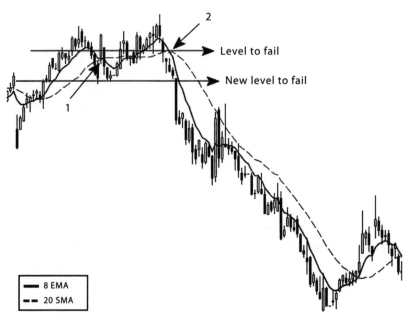

Figure 10.7 **Downside Pressure**

Figure 10.12 **Establish Behavior in the Bands**

Based on what we know about Bollinger bands, break that pencil out and mark on the chart in Figure 10.12 critical elements about the bands that you see here. Then, look at Figure 10.13 to see the things considered important to notice when trying to establish chart behavior in the bands.

1. We come upon the bands in a sideways formation, with a pierce at the top of the band. We know this implies rejection.
2. With parallel bands forming, this means our rejection of the top band sends us to test the bottom of the band (which it does).
3. Continual piercing of the lower band confirms strength of move, and sideways action again tells us change will be upon us.
4. The midline, the 25 SMA, provides us with adequate resistance and shows clear delineation of price at the bottom of the band.

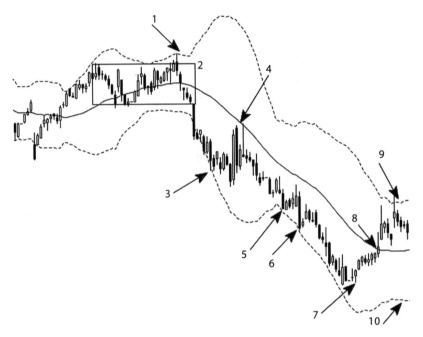

Figure 10.13 **Important Chart Points**

5. A piercing event occurs.
6. Another piercing event creates small reversal, as most piercings do.
7. Sideways action shows reversal potential.
8. Crossing of the midline occurs.
9. Piercing of the upper band occurs.
10. New parallel lines develop in the bands.

So how do we go back and begin this trade using the bands and minor elements of support and resistance?

Here, the Bollinger band expansion is the first trigger to go short. So we'll enter with our typical half size and set our stop at the midline of the bands, as seen in Figure 10.14.

That is quite close to the same entry point as the moving-average trade on our retry. Notice the arrows pointing to the bands

Figure 10.14 **Midline Stop**

are widening significantly, giving us the clear confirmation of momentum expansion.

Here's a question for you: what would you do if you had found this chart at the point of the oval in Figure 10.15?

Clearly you see momentum downward. What evidence or chart movement knowledge would you use to determine the movement of the stock, and what would you look for to go long? Do you see the sideways action I have highlighted with the rectangle? Normally, sideways action like this would give us the signal that a trade trigger would occur above the channel top to go long or below the channel bottom to go short, *but* what we are looking at here are Bollinger band formations, and if your memory holds from our conversations prior on the Bollinger bands, we'll see the pesky occurrence of a lower low that is not on the edge of the band. Again, when we see a lower low, but this lower low appears away from the edge of the band, there is a likelihood of a reversal in the current trend. This

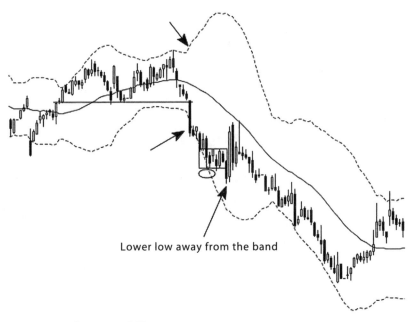

Lower low away from the band

Figure 10.15 **Downward Momentum**

reversal, or upside movement in our chart, does not trigger a high-probability long trade. What it does trigger is the alert for us to look for the failure of the corrective move so that we might return to our downtrend. This is the typical movement from waves and why we took the time to study them in chapters past.

Our decision should be to wait for the retracement to fail so that we might add and take a full position. Building on our techniques from the trades, if we are watching a bounce formation, where is it that we might assume it will fail? We know that the failure to breach prior to broken support (which has become new resistance) shows weakness of reversal, so we must have patience and watch for the failure—which comes to us at the topping-tail candle rejecting the midpoint (see the arrow in Figure 10.16).

To recap, the horizontal line identifies our stop as we continue to make lows. The arrow gives us a relative support region due to the bounce off the band. As you may recall, the moving averages gave us a very clean space to add to our short position, but as far as

Figure 10.16 **Stop and Relative Support**

I am concerned, the Bollinger bands do not have this power here in this particular chart. Due to the parameters we use to build the Bollinger bands, when we see an aggressive pullback into the lower bands, again, we will very often see a reversal.

Because countertrend moves, or reversals in a trend, can be slight to severe and can return to the prevailing trend quickly, a countertrend trade (for instance, going long on the bounce in a downward trending chart) provides a very low probability of success for the average trader. See how quickly the bounces retrace at arrows 5 and 6 in Figure 10.17.

Arrow 7 is important because it isolates the beginning of another sideways formation out from the edge of the band, suggesting the movement is taking a breath—or potentially staging a reversal. When sideways action like this occurs, keep a lookout for the appearance of a flattening bottom band, arrow 9. When the band flattens, the chance of reversal increases dramatically. As soon as the band flattens, we'll be looking for either the breach of prior resis-

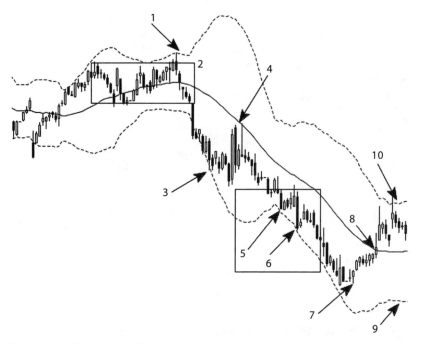

Figure 10.17 **Formation Points**

tance or the confirmation candle above the midpoint of the band, shown by arrow 8, which closely approximates the 20 SMA.

The confirmation candle here in our Bollinger band formation is nowhere near as good an exit as shown by the moving-average formations, but arrow 4 signals an area for us to add to the short. Where are we expecting this move to terminate? And why?

I'll answer this for you by asking you to look at what has happened to the Bollinger band formation, arrow 9. Notice the parallel formation that developed. Remember what happens to stock price in this environment? If it breached the top, as it did at arrow 10, it will test the bottom of the band.

As with our long trade, we leave the Bollinger band analysis seeing that the power lies in its ability to signal reversal points and extreme areas that make for excellent low-risk entries.

Fibonacci Retracements

Now for the Fibonaccis. Determining where to place the retracement levels is always going to be a skill only developed over time, a feel for the charts and an attention to wave patterns and chart strength. As a refresher, we desire to discover areas of extreme movement (fierce rejection or breakout represented by long wicks or large-range candle bodies) or heavy congestion (seen by continued sideways choppy action).

To reiterate, Fibs can be accurate if drawn congestion-to-congestion level; it is not only low to high. In order to draw the correct levels for the same chart, we'll need a 10,000-foot view with the Fibs drawn from an area of relative low congestion to relative high, as seen in Figure 10.18.

Fibs also do not make the most decisive trading rules when used without support. In my studies through the years, I see the

Figure 10.18 **Relative Chart High and Low**

Fibs as a topological map, but to navigate, we still need the additional tool or two. That being said, here is all we must assume in order to trade this chart short with only the Fibonaccis:

1. We assume we have drawn the correct Fibs.
2. We assume the trend is downward, which means that reversals to the upside seen in the chart will eventually fail.

That's it. Pretty simple premise, but if we are incorrect, it makes for a heap of worry—so although our parameter is a single one, it must be correct, or we will make a series of foolhardy trades.

Our trigger points will be the failure of support that our relative congestion has created, remembering that failure of congestion regions will be followed by a retest of that level. Knowing this, we'll need to be patient.

In Figure 10.19, the failure at point 1, the 38.2% level at 61.22, is the trigger to go short here, with the stop at 62.57. To be most conservative, enter at the retest of broken levels *unless* you have a great deal of volume or a breakaway formation. This formation was indeed a breakaway setup, so we took it at the first failure, knowing that there might have been the chance that we would test the stop level above.

So far, we notice that our Bollinger bands and Fibonacci levels both show us the same entry short, and the stop would be the Fib level above. Because we are forever concerned with the momentum sitting in a trade, the way we keep a close eye on this without the aid of moving averages or the bands is the measure and frequency of the failures to breach prior highs and the continued losses of new lows.

Since Fibs isolate important areas of support and resistance, they provide us with "stairs," just like our detailed view of the support and resistance in the long trade, that we can use as a continuing confirmation in strength of trend. As we mentioned in earlier chapters, understanding and isolating support and resistance will make a huge difference in your trading career if you do not currently employ this technique. It is invaluable as you trade from level to level to note

Figure 10.19 **Trigger Points**

any violations of support and resistance price levels. Something else I must reiterate: it is where the candle closes that determines whether the price level is broken or not. Though wicks should draw a raised eyebrow, the close of the candle is much more significant.

So we have entered short at the appropriate place and are now following the trade down. Where do we add to full size? The 61.8% retracement failure is an ideal level to do this. See area 2 in Figure 10.20. We'll shift our stop to the 50% retracement of 59.76. We will continue to trade down to each level and make a decision based on the environment to establish further trajectory.

Level 3 shows our first test of 100% retracement—this results in a bounce more than 85% of the time in a typical chart, so this is a key area to remove some of our gains as we are never quite sure how much of our chart we might retrace. So we'll take half of our gains

Figure 10.20 **Following the Trade Down**

off here at 53.59. Based on the chart action at the arrow, you can see that the break of the 100% level is not confirmed, and the lift here will stage our next addition of stock to the position. The most we expect that stock to retrace and still have a strong downward trend is the 61.8% Fib level. It does this but never closes the first candle above the level, implying weakness on the horizon. It is here at area 4 that we can add to the short position at 58.30, leaving our stop at 59.76.

Side note: What if we had shifted the stop down to 56.23? We would have been stopped out of the trade. Does being stopped out of a trade always imply that the trend is over and a reversal is on the way? No! If we see the stock advancing back to the 61.8%, it is here that we make the assessment of continuation.

Don't go looking for other trades when there is room to make more on the stock that already has your attention.

We would simply reenter the trade at the loss of level 4 in anticipation of retesting the 100% level. At the confirmation of the failure at level 5, we can shift our stop downward to 56.23. From here, we expect a test of the 138.2%, level 6, then 161.8%, level 7 if our trend continues. We can choose to shift our stop to 50.23 at the break of 47.42. Here again is where many of us begin to trim our positions when the charts say nothing about reversal. Granted, we cannot go broke taking profits, but we can deliver the wrong message to ourselves leaving money on the table, the message being, "Your timing is off. You just need to stay in." And like so much else we try to do when trading, we whitewash everything and end up sitting in trades that just eat us up.

Observe the next frame of observations in Figure 10.21. Losing the 161.8% retracement is a sign of huge weakness, and many times the loss of this level telegraphs the news that the 200% level is an

Figure 10.21 **Keep Following Down**

inevitability. Knowing this, once we clearly leave the 161.8 (or 61.8) level, shift the stop down to this point. It will become our new stop as we follow the trade down to the 200% level.

Another nuance here in Figure 10.21: do you see that we do not actually touch the 200% level? Instead, we stage a reversal just before it. When important levels such as 0, 50, 61.8, 100, 150, 161.8, 200, and so on, are approached and rejected just shy, it means that buyers were waiting at the level and moved quickly. We expect the bounce to test 178.6%, but the breach should move us to half size (unless we chose to take some right at the turn near the 200), and the recapture of the 161.8%, level 9 should make us close the trade. Notice, however, the chattering at 178.6%—this again is the sort of thing that disturbs the newer trader and makes for anxiety while holding. This behavior is the prelude to price resolution, and so we have to wait for the stock to break the relative highs (or lows) of nearby candles. Like I have mentioned many times, sideways action is a "sit on hands" event. Wait for the stock to tell you what it is going to do, and *wait* for the candles to tell you that the trade may be broken.

Three things I would like to reiterate when trading with Fibs. First, have patience and allow the stock to move where the Fibs suggest they will go. Second, paying attention to candle formations around these Fib levels will reveal future trajectory. Third, have patience. Oh yeah, I mentioned that already, even in the last chapter. Why mention it a dozen times? Because we won't, we simply won't have patience. Fear, angst, and dread will rip it from us. We'll forget our rules and where the indicators say we are going, take profits too quickly, or add in the wrong place because we don't wait for the candle to close.

Note to the trader: *You'd be surprised how much you'll make if you just forget about losing out.*

That's the bane of the trader's existence—being so afraid of losing out that we enter early trying to capture all the gains and leave late because we don't want to miss out in case it reverses.

Bringing Them All Together

There is a reason I only use a few technical indicators: the fewer the indicators, the less likely they disagree, and that means less indecision for me. As with the long trade, we'll now add all our pieces together and walk through the decision-making process involving all the indicators.

Now look at the chart in Figure 10.22. In order to be systematic, let's count the indicators as they occur—see how they follow through and create our system of measured stops as we walk through the trade.

Label 1 represents where we picked up the chart for review. As we begin looking for the best trading pattern to appear, we see a flat 20 SMA and two crossovers of the moving averages in close prox-

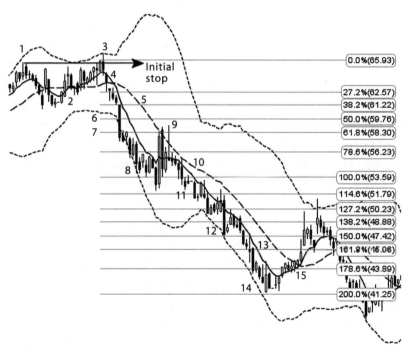

Figure 10.22 **All the Technicals Together**

frame. The trick becomes getting good at the setup and identification, then trusting oneself to allow the trade to follow through.

CONCLUSION

Let's write the sequence of the trade out. Our rules from our chapter on risk and setting trade size dictate that the initial stop always determines the size of our opening position. For sake of ease, let's just say that we'll hold a full size of 600 shares. Take another look at Figure 10.22. Our objective is to frame an appropriate trade and set its parameters for entry, size increase, stop loss, and exit. We will first notice that the chart is exhibiting channeling action, and we will trade the break of the channel.

1. First observation in the chart here to note a rejected high of 65.93.
2. Three simultaneous observations seen in this region: two moving average crossovers and reversal, and the hold of support at the 38.2% Fib of 61.22.
3. Second observation of a rejected high of 65.93.
4. Moving average crossover after second rejection of the high signals the shorting event at 63.23—short half size at 300 shares. Stop placed at 65.93.
5. Widening distance between moving averages and a loss of 61.22 signals the increase of size—short 300 more shares at 61.22. Shift stop to 63.53, just above first entry.
6. Swift failure of the 50% Fib at 59.76 signals the shift down on the stop loss to 61.22.
7. Failure of the 61.8% Fib suggests 100% retracement likely. Shift stop to 59.76.
8. Test, failure, and recovery of the 100% Fib signals the likelihood of 61.8% Fib retest.
9. Test and failure of the 61.8% Fib signals again a retest of the 100, as well as a shift down in the stop to 58.30 at the move back down.

10. Moving averages prove to be strong resistance here in the chart.

11. Retest and failure of the 100% Fib signals another shift down in the stop to 56.23.

12. Region here illustrates Bollinger band piercing behavior and bounce, as well as the test and rejection of the 138.2%. At this point, shift stop down to 50.23.

13. The golden ratio event touch at 161.8% signals removal of half size—buy to close 300 shares at 45.96 and shift stop down to 48.88.

14. Loss of the golden ratio and test of the 200% signals again removal of shares—buy to close 150 shares at 41.25. Shift stop down to 45.96.

15. Inflection signs for the first time since the trade began: Bollinger bands flattening, moving average crossover, and recovery of the 43.89 level at 178.6%. The position is closed here—buy to cover 150 shares at 43.89—prior to the stop due to signals appearing prior to test level.

OK, let's just take a breath for a minute before we continue. The next technical study, Chapter 12, will be more difficult as I am choosing a chart that many of us elect to trade but should not, and therefore open ourselves to difficulty that we don't need to manage during our day.

It is very taxing to read through these kinds of trade walk-throughs, especially if you are stopping to see what I am trying to point out—the evidence of how much attention and focus is necessary to trade with precision. It is a draining and continuously draining endeavor, but well worth it. So go through it again, see if you missed any of the finer points, and then begin to look at your own charts and replicate the event.

These are the types of things that we are not able to learn if we do not physically walk through our steps, and that will take work—and a lot of it.

10. Moving averages prove to be strong resistance here in the chart.

11. Retest and failure of the 100% Fib signals another shift down in the stop to 56.23.

12. Region here illustrates Bollinger band piercing behavior and bounce, as well as the test and rejection of the 138.2%. At this point, shift stop down to 50.23.

13. The golden ratio event touch at 161.8% signals removal of half size—buy to close 300 shares at 45.96 and shift stop down to 48.88.

14. Loss of the golden ratio and test of the 200% signals again removal of shares—buy to close 150 shares at 41.25. Shift stop down to 45.96.

15. Inflection signs for the first time since the trade began: Bollinger bands flattening, moving average crossover, and recovery of the 43.89 level at 178.6%. The position is closed here—buy to cover 150 shares at 43.89—prior to the stop due to signals appearing prior to test level.

OK, let's just take a breath for a minute before we continue. The next technical study, Chapter 12, will be more difficult as I am choosing a chart that many of us elect to trade but should not, and therefore open ourselves to difficulty that we don't need to manage during our day.

It is very taxing to read through these kinds of trade walk-throughs, especially if you are stopping to see what I am trying to point out—the evidence of how much attention and focus is necessary to trade with precision. It is a draining and continuously draining endeavor, but well worth it. So go through it again, see if you missed any of the finer points, and then begin to look at your own charts and replicate the event.

These are the types of things that we are not able to learn if we do not physically walk through our steps, and that will take work—and a lot of it.

Discipline, Dedication, and Endurance

"It was character that got us out of bed, commitment that moved us into action, and discipline that enabled us to follow through."

—ZIG ZIGLAR

Sometimes we treat discipline and dedication like four-letter words. In our microwave society, we want to do the very least to get the very most. The younger we are, it seems the easier we expect to achieve things. We want success yesterday, and many of us live with the dream of winning the lottery or a surprise inheritance. Trading particularly breeds this mindset, especially since, as I've mentioned, much of the marketing geared toward potential or actual retail traders aims to make trading appear simple and a bit foolproof. Nothing could be further from the truth, as many of us know, and we must clearly develop a set of skills in order to be competent and consistent. Two of these skills that have nothing to do with technique discussed so far are dedication and discipline.

Many of us choose to avoid dedication and discipline—it is why we have trouble with diet and exercise routines, or why we smoke or drink when part of us would like to stop, or why we shop too much, or give in to other excesses. We have a strong desire to give into self and enjoy what we want, exactly when we want it. But success in any difficult venue involves choices, and those choices often mean sacrifices are a part of our decisions. Take a look at any person at the pinnacle of what they do, and you will see a life of choices and sacrifice.

IT'S JUST A DECISION

If you are an accomplished musician, athlete, or in some specialized field, you know what I mean. Accomplishments of great measure will always come with a price, but these decisions are just made one at a time, and one day at a time. To pick dedication and discipline is as simple as saying, "I will." It comes one decision at a time, so it's best not to consider these things as some kind of anchor around our necks but instead as each decision taking us one step closer to our goals.

Evidence for Dedication

How does dedication show up in a trader's life? Dedication will show itself as a consistent commitment to understanding the markets and awareness of just how we are affected by it every day. The dedicated trader uses a journal, as discussed in Chapter 9, to chronicle the market and her actions through the day. The trader examines the market in different ways and makes the decision to learn something new every day that makes her a better person and a better trader. The dedicated trader studies after hours. She will review trades, scrutinize charts, and work to discover what she had missed during the work day. We need to ask ourselves what we use to measure "dedication." Trading is a craft, a specialized skill that needs to be honed, and the committed trader keeps her eyes on the grand objectives and aspirations—long-range success. Whatever manner

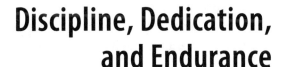

Discipline, Dedication, and Endurance

"It was character that got us out of bed, commitment that moved us into action, and discipline that enabled us to follow through."

—ZIG ZIGLAR

Sometimes we treat discipline and dedication like four-letter words. In our microwave society, we want to do the very least to get the very most. The younger we are, it seems the easier we expect to achieve things. We want success yesterday, and many of us live with the dream of winning the lottery or a surprise inheritance. Trading particularly breeds this mindset, especially since, as I've mentioned, much of the marketing geared toward potential or actual retail traders aims to make trading appear simple and a bit foolproof. Nothing could be further from the truth, as many of us know, and we must clearly develop a set of skills in order to be competent and consistent. Two of these skills that have nothing to do with technique discussed so far are dedication and discipline.

Many of us choose to avoid dedication and discipline—it is why we have trouble with diet and exercise routines, or why we smoke or drink when part of us would like to stop, or why we shop too much, or give in to other excesses. We have a strong desire to give into self and enjoy what we want, exactly when we want it. But success in any difficult venue involves choices, and those choices often mean sacrifices are a part of our decisions. Take a look at any person at the pinnacle of what they do, and you will see a life of choices and sacrifice.

IT'S JUST A DECISION

If you are an accomplished musician, athlete, or in some specialized field, you know what I mean. Accomplishments of great measure will always come with a price, but these decisions are just made one at a time, and one day at a time. To pick dedication and discipline is as simple as saying, "I will." It comes one decision at a time, so it's best not to consider these things as some kind of anchor around our necks but instead as each decision taking us one step closer to our goals.

Evidence for Dedication

How does dedication show up in a trader's life? Dedication will show itself as a consistent commitment to understanding the markets and awareness of just how we are affected by it every day. The dedicated trader uses a journal, as discussed in Chapter 9, to chronicle the market and her actions through the day. The trader examines the market in different ways and makes the decision to learn something new every day that makes her a better person and a better trader. The dedicated trader studies after hours. She will review trades, scrutinize charts, and work to discover what she had missed during the work day. We need to ask ourselves what we use to measure "dedication." Trading is a craft, a specialized skill that needs to be honed, and the committed trader keeps her eyes on the grand objectives and aspirations—long-range success. Whatever manner chosen to define dedication, it must hold the crucial component of always moving us up to the next rung.

A Focus on Discipline

Discipline is not dedication; but a disciplined person will be dedicated. Once we establish the need for dedication and implement it, we'll need to direct our energy to remaining dedicated to our pursuits and plans day after day. Dedication is much simpler to achieve than discipline because discipline is organized routine. It infers purpose and direction in a consistent fashion. Routine, however, is a bit boring for most of us, especially if we have the personality of the typical person drawn to the markets to trade, but it is absolutely necessary for achievement here. Consistent discipline infers a need for endurance, and mental endurance cannot be understated at all. The market will beat us into submission if we give it the chance.

EMOTIONAL EXHAUSTION

It feels like I've been trading for fifty years. I look in the mirror sometimes and think it might be a hundred. Seriously. Instead, it's only been about six. In that short time, I have seen a lot of people drop out of trading; sometimes it takes a few months, sometimes a year or two, but eventually way too many of us become lunch for the market's voracious appetite. It's a brutal place, the market, stripping us of cash, confidence, and courage. But you know that already if you're taking the time to read this book.

When we, the average retail traders, enter the short-term swing-trading/day-trading world, we usually have such grand hopes. Some of us are hopelessly overly optimistic about achievement, thinking that in spite of our limited trading knowledge, we'll "wing it" and somehow we'll make out like Steve Cohen. Some of us are just hopeful that we can have some success as we learn. But most, if not all, retail traders are woefully lacking in the skill necessary to achieve victory in the market.

Did our initial actions set us up to be a market statistic, one of the people who fell by the wayside and never made a career out of trading, leaving the endeavor with nothing more than depleted portfolio holdings? Tragically, most of us will fail with our limited opening skill sets; the probability of success does not remotely sit in our favor. From my reckoning, it seems that for every fifty traders I see, only one will I see a year later, and yet, though we may enter the game behind the eight ball, we can still ultimately choose whether we succeed or fail. Our choices, once we enter the mysterious and alluring world, will determine that for us. The power to succeed sits squarely on our shoulders.

Trading is not about acting on the next big tip from someone "important," or buying hot stocks; it is not about understanding macroeconomic theory; it is not about company fundamentals, or technical systems; it is not about great trading methods; it is not about finding the next guru online and following what he or she seems to do. Trading is all about the individual; the choices of the individual supply the reason for success or failure. I focus a lot on my personal experiences in this book as we journey together because it is my understanding that many of us come up the same way. The prod to investigate our insides will be strong since this is where we will need the most work. The explanation of the skill necessary may be simple, but our personality and our internal mechanisms that call us to action will forever be a workspace for each of us.

BREAKING YOUR RULES

Sometimes the tendency toward tunnel vision as a day trader can be astounding. We can be very knowledgeable on every rule and know many different alerts, formations, and triggers, but somehow in the middle of our day, we'll become focused on one thing, and we'll ignore everything else as the trade continues. We'll end up breaking three other rules so that the one rule upon which we are focused holds true. Who has done that? (Yes, I see your hands up everywhere—don't even try to keep yours down.) This happens to the best of us. I believe it has to do with the fact that trading brings us into focus on something that we equate to our profit and loss, and in doing this, it skews our ability to clearly see all the signs out there.

We trade according to a bias; it is a necessity, but how heavily we allow the bias to influence us is a measure of our strength as a technical analyst. No matter how long we trade, we will battle every day with separating a trade into the parts we think and the parts we see, because (and here's the rub) they are readily intertwined.

NOW, WHERE IS THAT HAMMER?

And not the rubber kind, either. When I err on the side of shifting my bias in the wrong direction—the direction I think or believe to be true but does not corroborate with a series of technical indicators—and make a poor or hasty trade, I will remark to those who work with me, "I'm looking for a hammer" (to smash my fingers for making the bad trade). I began using an "ice pick to the temple" analogy, but luckily I have never experienced that firsthand. I have, however, smashed myself with a hammer a time or two by accident! Interestingly, this vivid and admittedly horrifying vision actually works as I try to trade.

I don't mentally beat myself up (not too much at least), but I allow myself to feel the "penalty" that helps me trade better the next time around. I equate the poor trade not only with opportunity cost and monetary loss, but also to a physical and physiological element that allows me to respond as I see that hammer coming down on my fingers. Though it may seem strange to you now, the more conscious you become of your emotions and emotional states, and the more willing to train yourself up psychologically to trade well, the better you will trade and the less likely you are to continually make the same mistakes over and over again.

Do you ever say to yourself, "Why in the world am I always making that mistake?" The answer is twofold actually: one reason is that you have trained yourself to respond to the wrong cues, this being the rational element; and the second is that, at the end of the day, you have not anchored a truly distasteful memory to your actions. I hear ya, I know it seems odd, but I assure you, it works. I believe the psychological term is *aversion behavior therapy*, and it is most effective.

IF IT'S TO BE, IT'S UP TO ME

There's a lot of responsibility to bear in this profession, and frankly, quite a few of us are unwilling to step up to that level of accountability. Most of us are adrift in the stream; looking at too much, learning too little, and losing money while the market tries to teach lessons that few seem to pay attention to well enough to learn. It is often on Fridays that these thoughts come to me, as I see folks end another week no more successful than the last one and still thinking that they are a razor's edge from "getting it": part dismal, part hopeful about next week being different.

We don't look with a detailed eye at the week's past trades to see where *our decisions* were wrong, but instead, blame it on market conditions, bad luck, manipulation, timing, whatever, just not ourselves or our selection process. Then, without a thought of how to really attack the true nature of the problem, we look into next week, not realizing that we are doomed to repeat the mistakes of the prior one because of the inability to change the way we make decisions.

We all know that the market is a tough place to work, and many of us are in the treading-water business, barely keeping our heads above the line. Some of us do well, but we also have those days that just seem like every time we step into a trade, we're standing on a trapdoor with a noose around our neck, ready to hang at the release of the latch. OK, that was a bit graphic, but the shock of being on the wrong side of a trade when I'm carrying size always seems to feel like that no matter how many gains I've banked for the week. It's like the fear and dread of trading as a novice comes back to slap me in the face.

I would venture to say, if we were all truthful, those of us who have been weather beaten by the market still come face to face with these reminders of how quickly, without risk management, we can be reduced to ashes. The management of risk will be the cornerstone of a fruitful trading career.

Decision Making

The market promises us, if we don't get how this "trading thing" works, we will lose enough money to leave and never come back. A direct promise—a threat, even. Some of us will read that statement with a sick feeling in our stomach, knowing it might be us the market delivers that promise to, but even though we feel that way, most of us who are determined will get up on Monday and perform the same mistakes we made last Monday. Even though we will study and focus on this technical or that, this fundamental or that, and swear to ourselves that we will do better, in the end, we'll log another dreadful week in the market, all because we did not change the appropriate behavior.

Here's a question: you know how sometimes we think we know what to do in certain situations; and, indeed, if we are quizzed, we will answer correctly—but when the actual event comes, we will make the wrong decision? A snap decision turns out to be the wrong one, and if we evaluate it afterward, we say, "I knew that. Now, why did I make the wrong choice?" Simply knowing the right thing to do does not make it a given that we will do the right thing. How true that statement is in everything. If we understand this is true in ordinary situations, what makes us think that we are somehow immune from doing that in the high-stress world of trading?

Yet, we don't think about this situation very much at all because we mistakenly assume that trading is a mechanical process, only governed by systems. The governing body, however, is the human mind, and it is engineered differently from profitable trading systems. I asked a student of mine whether he would mind if I used a question from our conversation as the springboard to the

188 THE TRADING BOOK

following discussion, and he graciously agreed, so I'll recap what was said.

He asked, "Why is it that I can see what to do, and I know what to do, but when it comes to the execution of the event, I fall on my face in the trade?" I responded quickly by answering, "The *only* answer there, I am afraid, is that there is a problem with the triggers to the decision, with the way problems are approached, and the mechanics used to make decisions. When you and I make decisions, we will first mentally make them, then physically execute them, and the only way to change that is, well, by change, manifested in behavior modification." There has to be a step in between the mental assessment and the physical execution, and it should be a verification. It will help determine the strength of the mental decision.

Try as we might, our primal state is to resist change and to be unwilling to accept the unfamiliar; so by nature, *most* will trade in the same way we function in our lives—viscerally—by gut and emotion. Emotion is the part of our being that preserves us, so we will get out of some painful situation before we "feel" it will deliver maximum hurt levels. If we make decisions in our lives through any other process, it is because we have learned it. Look at any child to determine whether this is true.

Trading, on the other hand, necessitates we learn to control this instinctive element about ourselves; eliminate it from our general processes in this world—and stand in the face of fire if we have a good plan.

Patience

Here's a direct example of a very difficult trading event of 2010, and evidence of the need to stand and take the heat. To quickly recap, I was in a naked short NFLX strangle (it is as risky a trade as it sounds) into earnings, and it gapped significantly against me at the open. For those who are not familiar with this trading strategy, it is best suited when the estimation of movement is slight to negligible—but extremely dangerous if a stock has a sizable run in either direction if the strikes for the options are too close. It was a particularly grueling trade that left me considerably under water at the open, and continued to run up against me, naturally. With mounting losses, I shared with the trading room what I was doing, vocalizing my internal dialogue and decision-making process, and as I worked through the tight trade, a number of my colleagues commented (some publically, some privately) that the patience I exhibited in my trade in the face of sizable loss was a key learning event of the day. The question is, *how* could I be patient?

Obviously, the trade did not seem to be going in my favor at the open, so it wasn't positive reinforcement from gains. It wasn't the market going up, as it was in a downward to flat holding pattern. It wasn't the slope of the trend, as momentum seemed to flatten right after I entered the trade. So what was it? What was it that led me to hold the position longer, to give it a little more room, to shift the stop a little lower, and to wait, rather than leave the position underwater?

I don't want to get bogged down in the details of the trade here, because I am focusing not on the skills of observation about the technical but about the patience waiting for the trade to develop. The bottom line, as many of you know who followed me live in the Twitter stream or in the trading room directly, is that I went from a –$7,250 position to a $4,370 when it was all said and done—an $11K swing on the trade. However, if I had left the position the way it was at its nadir, I would have closed the position at the end of the day down more than $9K.

Though I did not relish the predicament I was in, I was prepared not to tuck tail and run, because I had a plan. Most of us in this kind of danger without training and preparation would retreat and take cover—instinctively. If a bear rushes at us, our minds do not say to stand and fight (the market rushes at us with this level of ferocity many times) but to run. The unprepared mind has a tendency to freeze due to *indecision*, frozen without a thought of what to do next in the trade, and this normally leads to a market mauling, claws and all.

Before I began to follow a stringent set of guidelines, I had been mauled many, many (did I mention many) times by the market while I stood frozen deciding what to do. If I had not really understood the rhythm that NFLX was in, had I not possessed the tools to negotiate myself out of the particular trade, I would have not had the patience nor the calm of purpose to wrangle myself out of it and still leave with gains.

This is the space we should aspire to be in—always ready for what might come, surprised by nothing, prepared for everything. The only way to reach this space is through planning and provision *before* we enter the market, realizing, as Ben Franklin said, "He that can have patience, can have what he will."

INCREASING COMPETENCY IN DECISION MAKING

We all know that good trading systems have rules, and those rules need to be followed, but we either forget the rules or choose not to follow them due to the dramatic effect on our psyche when we are faced with a situation for which we did not prepare. This shock to our system is the foundation for irrational trading, and the only way to better decision making is the eradication of this shock treatment our mind delivers. Not only do we have to become better decision makers, we have to do it in an emotionally exhausting environment fraught with trials and disappointment. A tall order. That's why we pick up trading books, join mailing lists, and sign up for webinars. We recognize that we need the information to assist us in making decisions, but we forget that, in themselves, facts and figures do not make us better decision makers.

My counsel to you is this: think carefully about what makes you act. Open that trading journal; write what makes you jump; try to recall things that come to mind about your mental state at the execution of such a trade. Reference emotion, level of anxiety, regret, and anything else you felt at the time. Record which mistakes you seem to most often make and pinpoint what emotional trigger is driving the incorrect response. Is the trigger one of the four monsters of emotional trading: fear, desperation, anger, or greed? Our primary psychological objective is to isolate those components of our personality that play the part of hijacker to our desired achievement, quarantine the behaviors, and short-circuit the triggers that cause them.

We're all going to make bad trades; there are no perfect traders, and there are no perfect systems. The strongest mindset comes from those who are willing to work at being better than they were yesterday. The golden rule is this: the market is a living, breathing, and moving thing, and if you think you have arrived, it won't be long before you are watching it pass you by. Use aversion therapy. Pick anything—a car door slam, stubbing your toe against a piece of furniture, drinking orange juice after brushing your teeth—something that takes control of your physical state so that you might become more aware of the decision you are about to make. And remember, trading well is all about your ability to make good decisions in front of your screen.

CONCLUSION

I find it interesting that none of us would argue with the need for patience, discipline, and dedication, but few of us take the extra step to enforce and foster these traits within ourselves—whether reaching for a box of donuts or cigarettes or while trading. I surmise that lack of effort has to do with the difficulty associated with the consistency needed for such actions to become habitual. The same is true about self-exploration and personal behavior assessment. In reading and watching interviews of other accomplished traders, I have heard them say, "Good trading made me a better person," and I used to wonder what that meant. Then I realized that the traits that build good traders are the traits that build good people. The choice to embark on the road to excellence, however, by sheer definition, implies additional effort on many fronts, and the more we learn about ourselves and the market, the more patient we become—waiting for the moments that make for the best trades. It is only in those high-probability opportunities that we will find, through the development of these discussed skills, our path to true trading strength and the additional benefit of personal development.

CHAPTER 12

The Ideal Trade Setup

"Half of the failures in life come from pulling one's horse
when he is leaping."

—THOMAS HOOD

Defining the edge means defining the trade. Without probability stacked in our favor, we may as well be rolling dice or "pulling the horse." For those of us less familiar with jumping, pulling the horse means tightening on the reins while the horse is either just about to jump or in the immediate moments at the point of the jump. This telegraphs uncertainty to the horse, and the horse will not jump cleanly or with certainty if he believes his rider is not confident that he can carry through. Horses have a keen sense of intuition and need to feel that their rider has dominion over the environment, or they will perform poorly. I saw a rider pull a horse once while attempting a jump. Ugly!

Many of us jump into trades without a trading edge, then we pull the horse—we hesitate and reevaluate due to fear and indecision. We leave the trade early or make unwise decisions in the process of the trade, and we end up in a tangled mess. Unfortunately, many of us are unclear on what a trading edge actually is, or if we do understand the concept, we are unclear on how to define it.

I like to outline the elements of a clear trading edge, and, as a result, I can find a great trading entry and probable exit. An edge can be expressed as something that gives us a step-up on our opponent or competitor, akin to a loading of the dice or stacking of the deck, but entirely acceptable in the market. The edge will demarcate the opening of the position. Most traders and investors start at a relatively arbitrary level—the "this looks good" level—possibly because someone recommends a stock or it may just have come to the radar and the chart seems strong. To best our competition, we'll have to do just a little more (it really does take only a little more) than they do, and that means we seek out the space that gives us the advantage.

DEFINING THE EDGE

Momentum is one of the most clearly defining trading edges, but sharp momentum will not make your trade a guaranteed success. Simply because a stock is moving straight up doesn't mean it is safe to enter. Before we enter any trade, we must isolate a potential strategy. If our strategy is trading momentum, as it is with our market positioning system, we must isolate a stock with room to move. We know from our study of moving averages that momentum is seen with the steepness of slope and that the greater the volume, the higher the likelihood of momentum advancement. Always focus on this element of your charts—the slope effect is the wind at our backs. Though volume does not definitively dictate length or strength of move, it does help with determining how quickly a correction might or might not occur. Low volume equals high probability of return or correction.

Additionally, sufficient volume, though often ignored by novice traders, is a must. Volume means liquidity; and liquidity means that we are able to name our price. A lack of liquidity means that we are at the mercy of the market makers, and we might be left holding shares we cannot sell or being short shares we cannot buy to close.

A minimum of 500,000 shares average daily volume traded is acceptable—any less, and we run the risk of being unable to exit or enter at our predetermined time and price because there is no one sitting on the other side of our trade.

The strength of a chart is also vital. Very simply, a chart is strong if the waves are rhythmic and organized, does not gap much, and if it does gap, it retraces nicely. It clearly breaks out of high-probability formations like channels and pennants, and the Fib levels are clean, which means the stock does not spend a lot of time in congestion along Fib level. Messy charts involving sideways movement and gappy action cause an element of uncertainty that we need to eradicate when defining our edge and moving toward a decision.

The "beta" of a stock, or the ratio at which it moves relative to the broad market, is central to the day trader. Stocks with low betas are stocks that slowly trend in one direction or another and rarely break formation. They lack evidence of momentum with slight sloping charts. These kinds of instruments belong in a very low risk portfolio, not concerned with volatility or capturing the magic of momentum.

SOLIDIFY THE TRADING TIME FRAME AND FIND THE PREVAILING TREND

Trading the daily? Make sure the weekly and the four-hour charts are following the same trend, or about to resume. Trading the four-hour chart? Make sure the daily and hourly charts are following the same trend, or about to resume. Trading the 15-minute chart? Make sure the hourly and 5-minute charts are following the same trend. For trading the 5-minute chart, make sure the 15- and 2-minute charts are following the same trend. These tight trading levels are best suited to the more experienced, so if possible, try to trade longer time frames until a deeper understanding of chart, candlestick, and technical formations comes.

It is surprising how many trades we get excited about just plain fail this simple test to confirm the strength of a trend using the multiple time frames. If the stock in consideration does have similar trends across time frames and if the stock tells the same story, the chart has a very high probability of continuation, and that means trading success. The rule of thumb again is, the more the time frames coincide, the greater the chance for victory over the market.

We don't *have* to trade *something*. Learn to wait for the kill. Which is better? Three trades that make $5,000 or 20 trades that make $5,000 but lose $4,000 before we recover? Our goal is to be in the market for as little time as possible at the most strategic price and at the most conducive place and time to create success. We are not in the "throw spaghetti against the wall to see what sticks" game. We're calculating professionals.

The less skill we have, the more likely it is that we will stay in trades hoping for the big move, and this can be incredibly detrimental to success. I heard an analyst once say on one of these television stations that a person had to stay in the market because the real major moves occur about 5 to 10 days out of a year, and we needed to wait around for them (no doubt trying to convince folks not to liquidate their accounts). She's probably in another career since she was working for Lehman at the time. However, some people would firmly agree with this statement. I do not. Sitting fully invested in the market is about as appealing to me as licking pavement—not at all, in case you wondered. The years 2007 to early 2010 gave me that lesson. If I were not skilled and not able to capitalize on daily moves, I might feel differently, but I have a great sense of comfort keeping myself in high levels of cash at the end of each day. Not to say I do not stay in the market, but I am most eager to get off the train when I see it slowing.

Here's a confession of epic magnitude. When I first started trading, I did not know one solitary thing about time frames and how technical indicators shift between time frames, nor did I know how to establish prevailing trends, and *that* made for a ton of bad trades. A good number of newer retail traders do not understand the concept of time frames, and even after coming into contact with the concept, when and what to trade still confuses many. I'd like to take a moment here to look at our technicals and see just how perspective changes as we consider time frames. Because the best momentum trades are made in the direction of the strongest trend, it is our primary goal to estimate what direction that actually is. The next three frames, Figures 12.1–12.3, are illustrations of the same chart. The question then becomes what, if any, directional trades exist in each of the charts?

Figure 12.1 is a chart of five-minute candles. From our studies, we know that a trade does exist to go long above the congestion of the right side of the chart—there is a clear channel defined there, and we can trade to the last relative high in the stock at left. If it breaks out of that channel, that prior top becomes the most likely target. What can we say about force of movement from the volume chart? Minimal. Not really a trade that I am too keen on taking. What is the slope of the Bollinger band? Flat. What about the moving averages? Flat. Decision? No trade right now.

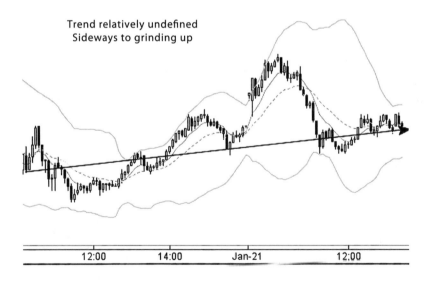

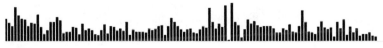

Figure 12.1 **Five-Minute Candles**

How about the chart in Figure 12.2? The stock in Figure 12.2 is the same one as shown in Figure 12.1, but we are reviewing the daily candles instead of the five-minute ones. That sideways movement in the tight time frame becomes more colorful in the larger chart assessment. Could we assume that the drift up on the five-minute chart might be more reliable since the daily is uptrending? What do we notice, however, that might be a little troubling about the long here? How about the slope of the Bollinger bands? Downward sloping. Those moving averages? Flat. Though this is an uptrending stock, what is the trending direction from the highs to the last print to the right? See the lower highs and lower lows? That is a downtrend in development. So we see a slight uptrend in the five-minute chart and a new downtrend development in the daily chart.

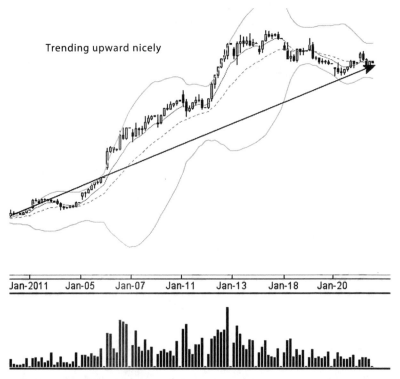

Figure 12.2 **Daily Candles**

Our technical indicators are less than decisive. Decision? No good trade exists.

Let's look at another frame of reference in Figure 12.3. This weekly chart shows extreme parabolic expansion and a bull flag pulling away from the upper band. Why would we not short this, or then again, why might we? What would we have to see to assist us in making a decision? Take a look at those Bollinger bands: sharp upside acceleration. It could mean parabolic exhaustion, but the stock might be just taking a breath. Steep slope on those moving averages with volume continuation looks very good for further upside if we are going to take a swing long position in the stock. The diminishing volume on the pullback is also a good sign that the stock might recover nicely.

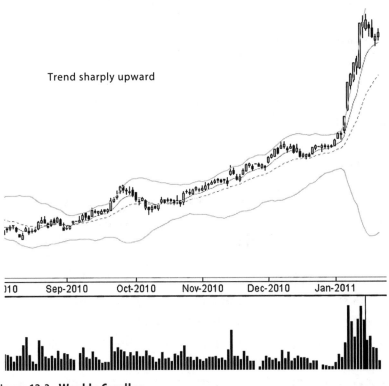

Figure 12.3 **Weekly Candles**

Bull flags should not be shorted, by and large, as they are against the prevailing trend, but so long as the candles resist the top of the chart, the downward trend will continue. Another reason we would be wise not to short this would be the observance of the 8 EMA holding as support below the candles above. We are very eager to make risky trades because our natural minds somehow pick for us the desire to trade countertrend trades. Whatever the case, be warned not to do this. It will devastate our accounts over time.

That stock was pretty simple to analyze. Why? Because it was sharply trending and the pattern was very sturdy. These are the kinds of stocks that we like to trade—whether up or down, they need to look tidy. We often make trading unnecessarily difficult for ourselves because we choose the wrong vehicle in which to trade. Stack the deck by always attempting to work with those stocks that pattern well. We need to look for the Maybachs and trade them: the very worst for going short, and the very best for going long.

When we have signals that are either noncommittal or swiftly reversing, we expose ourselves to an environment where we are constantly second-guessing ourselves. That alone can destroy any chances of capturing gains.

THE 15-MINUTE RULE

The 15-minute rule is remarkably simple, short, and sweet, but it will save us from a catastrophe of trades if we pay close attention. When the market opens, there is always a pent-up number of buyers and sellers waiting to get in. Sometimes, the spikes or dips come from houses jockeying funds around or perhaps the orders that come in from the retail trader who sees that an alert has been triggered. Whatever the case, there is a high probability of price reversal at the open of the day. The stock will either spike up or dip down, but by the time the first 15 minutes are over, a trend has usually been set. Of course, a trend could be negative, positive, or nonexistent—but within this time frame, the stock often shows its hand.

The rule is extremely reliable and valid if both the 8 EMA and the 20 SMA moving averages have slope (evidence of sustainable momentum on the time frame chosen to trade). It says the following:

- If a stock breaches the high of the first 15-minute candle at any time after that during the trading day and the stock shows momentum, i.e., slope in the moving averages, the price will continue in the direction above.
- If a stock breaks the low of the first 15-minute candle at any time after that during the trading day, and the stock shows momentum, i.e., slope in the moving averages, the price will continue in the direction below. To verify this, open any chart on the 5-minute time frame. Remember that a 15-minute high could be made at the opening price print—and the same goes for the low.

Make sure to keep this in mind when you are getting set up for your daily trading activities. Pay close attention and reap the rewards.

CHECKLIST PRIOR TO ENTERING A TRADE

The following list should be considered before you enter a trade. Though it is a conservative action, it will lead you to the highest chances of success.

1. We must qualify the stock.
   a. The stock must have high liquidity—this means >500,000 shares traded daily.
   b. The stock should have stable price patterns—this means few gaps or no unfilled gaps and with a good linear trend.
   c. The stock should present a clear trending pattern.
   d. It is imperative to be keenly aware of earnings releases or conferences before you enter the trade, and not after your proposed entry.

2. Pick the time frame to trade the stock, and make sure the larger and smaller time frames show the same type of trend. Conflict creates confusion, so eliminate conflict.
3. Identify the best trend to trade within the stock, and note the slope and Bollinger band locations.
4. Identify any nearby high-volume areas or volatile or reversal candle formations, and highlight them on the stock chart.
5. Once the stock has been isolated, draw the weekly, daily, and four-hourly Fibs, and delete the ones the chart has told you are unimportant.
6. Isolate the probable target entry for the trade, either at the breach of a nearby Fib or moving-average formation.
7. Recognize that premium long-target entries are usually found when the stock price is bouncing off support levels, not breaking over resistance.
8. Recognize that premium short-target entries are usually found when the stock price is rejecting the resistance levels, not breaking through support.
9. Isolate the probable target exit for the trade, and set an alert just before the price event so that you'll be prepared for the exit.
10. Pinpoint the relative stop if you are day- or swing-trading (use daily or four-hourly candles to establish stops if you are swing-trading), and mark it clearly on your charts and set alerts just before it so that you are ready and aware when the event is about to occur.
11. Calculate the total acceptable risk exposure for your trade—that number, as you may recall, is the number of shares you hold multiplied by the distance from your entry point and your stop.
12. Wait for the confirmation candle to complete if using the moving averages to trade. If Fibs are being used, it is best to isolate a breakout formation around the level if there is congestion or to go to the time frame just beneath the

one chosen to trade to see the break above or below just a little earlier.

13. To be most conservative, make sure that none of your trades are opened in the first 15 minutes, and keep an eye on the high and low made in the first 15 minutes, as these levels will prove out to be quite important during the day.

14. As soon as new areas of relative support or resistance form, raise the stops and take the opportunity to either add or remove from the position, but keep the risk threshold always in sight to make sure your rules are not violated.

15. At the probable target, remove some of the position; the choice will be individual to continue forward in hopes the stock will continue in the direction of the trend, but greed is often a great factor when evaluating losses. Many great trades have been reduced to being nominal by failing to remove some of the position.

This MPS system is a simple, systematic, and structured approach for the identification and execution of the ideal high-probability trade for any instrument in the market—stock, futures, forex (currency), and even options when trading chart momentum. Consistently executed, the results are nothing short of astounding. But, as with all excellent trading systems, there is always the linch-pin for profit—the human discretionary element and the associated skill on board. YOU!

DAILY PREPARATION ROUTINE

Never underestimate the power of preparation—when we are pre-pared, we manage the unexpected with greater skill. The market, in case you forgot, is filled with unforeseen events, and being off our game is the worst space to be in when we trade.

In addition to the trade-entering checklist, the following add-on list is always good to run through as well. I find that the more

I jump through these hoops, the more lucrative the day is. Work on getting better than anyone around at following a routine checklist. Me, I assume I am a surgeon, and life and death hang in the balance. Though it might sound draconian, it keeps me out of bad trades. Be well aware that given over to itself, the mind behaves most irrationally.

- Have you checked the economic calendar today?
- Does your stock have any conference calls scheduled?
- Are any of your holdings close to earnings?
- Have you looked to the long-term trend *today* to see if anything changed from yesterday?
- Any unusual volume disappearing or showing up?
- Do your moving averages have slope on the time frame you are trading?
- Are you near a Fib level?
- Are your moving averages above or below the candles printing?
- Does your Bollinger band have slope?
- Where is your stock in relation to the Bollinger bands?
- Have your candles pierced the Bollinger bands?
- Are you in a low-volatility area that might whip you around?
- Is it the first 15 minutes of the day?
- Have you set a reasonable stop?
- Have you determined your maximum loss exposure?
- Do you have an exit price?
- Do you have an entry price?
- When will you know when the trade is broken?
- When will you know when the trend is reversing?
- Is this a low-probability trade?
- Is this a high-probability trade?
- Is your stock moving above, below, or through the golden ratio?
- Have you determined what is most likely?
- Is your trade aligned with what is most likely? Why not?

- What time frame are you trading?
- Can you tell by candlesticks when a stock is going to reverse?
- Are there any glaring formations that could ruin your trade?
- Is there nearby overhead support or resistance?
- Are you prepared for the worst-case scenario?
- If you are in a trade going poorly, was it an impulse trade?
- Are you trading trend or countertrend?

I understand these are a lot of questions to consider, but the less we leave to chance in the realm of possibilities, the smaller the risk, the greater we are able to size our trade, and the greater the chance of superior returns. Will all of those questions make us not trade a lot of things? Yes, but if we traded them anyway, and lost, which of those options would be more favorable to us?

CONCLUSION

The granularity with which we choose to observe the trading landscape is in direct proportion to the control we exercise over our trades. The more control we take, the more comfortable we become taking trades. That comfort level in its own right will assuage so many fears we carry with us to the trading world. In your trade ideal setup, you must:

- Define and understand your trading edges, keeping in mind that momentum is by far one of the most important.
- Solidify the trading time frame while looking for the prevailing trend. Consider the charts in this chapter to help improve your frame of reference when trading.
- Keep the 15-minute rule in mind at the outset of your trading day.
- Refer back to the checklists in this chapter to lead you to your highest chances of success. Whether technical or emotional, these questions will undoubtedly aid in your improvement.

The fight to establish control in trading is paramount to success, and the direct path to that is by the strict enforcement of rules and regimens that "corner" the choices our stocks will make. If we give our trades only one way to go, and it goes another, that makes life very simple. Either the stock does what we want it to when we want it to, or we'll drop it and look for another time or stock that will comply to *our* rules of engagement. When we are selective, we are always better for it—in any aspect of our lives.

CHAPTER 13

Nuances of
Chart Formations

"That which we persist in doing becomes easier, not that the task itself has become easier, but that our ability to perform it has improved."

—RALPH WALDO EMERSON

In trading we are often made very conscious of the fact that even though events seem similar, they often are telling a different story. The process of analyzing charts is a highly contextual endeavor and somewhat like learning a new language. Therefore, a closer look at some related patterns is needed.

IN THE WEEDS: SIMILAR FORMATIONS

The greatest difficulty about trading well is knowing when situations differ. Because I find the channel to be a remarkably sound pattern to trade, we're going to spend some time in the finer details of decision making in the trade. I'd like to start with two patterns that begin the same way.

First, take a look at Figure 13.1. Sometimes traders will designate this kind of pattern as a bull flag because it is a downward trending channel in an upward trending chart. Our challenge is to decide what to do at the break of the channel boundaries. Do we go long on the reversal as we breach the top, do we go short as it breaks the lower channel line, or do we do something entirely different relative to what else we see?

To be a superior trader, we must plan for each scenario that might occur when we are looking for an alert to signal a trade entry. We are going to leave the Fibonacci directional help out here so we

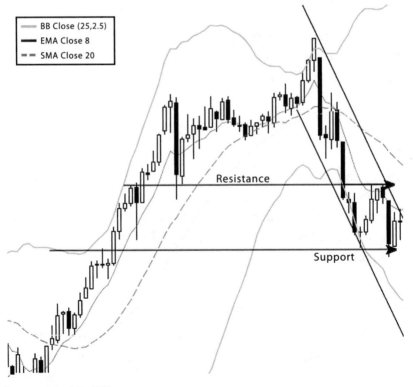

Figure 13.1 **A Bull Flag**

can focus only on the formations in front of us. With support and resistance as shown in Figure 13.1, what kind of mental dialogue and trade setup strategy do we need?

First, we're trading the channel break in any direction for continuation in the direction of the break. What might be signaling a break is on the horizon?

- Sideways movement on the Bollinger band
- No new lows in the sideways movement

The stock in the chart looks like it might break upside. We do not immediately act every time it breaks. Instead, we look for signs that the break has continuation potential. What might continuation potential look like?

- Broken overhead resistance, or lower-level support
- Moving averages have slope, both the 8 and the 20
- Moving averages show inflection or continuation, depending on the direction of the break
- Confirmation candle in the direction of the trade
- Though not pictured, higher volume levels on the breakout signify strong likelihood of continuation

Figure 13.2 shows what transpired. We're breaking upside. What signals do we have to go long?

- Broken out above top channel trend line
- Confirmation candle outside the top channel trend line
- Confirmation candle printing above the 8 EMA
- Candles bouncing from support making higher highs and higher lows

Looks good to go long, huh? Wait a second. What signals in Figure 13.2 show that this breakout might fail? (Note: always con-

Figure 13.2 **Breaking Upside**

sider the evidence that suggests the analysis is wrong and weigh that against the opposing analysis before deciding what to do.)

- 20 SMA above is resistance
- Price-level resistance above
- Rejection of the price-level resistance
- Long is a countertrend trade

Though it seems there are more reasons to go long here, the main reason to wait for more confirmation is daunting, namely *price rejection*. Price rejection trumps all other signals, so we need to wait for the breach and confirmation candle above our labeled resistance point, and then over our 20 SMA.

Figure 13.3 **Overhead Resistance Holds**

OK, so what happened in Figure 13.3? Well, that would be nothing, which is why waiting for confirmation is so important. Still, overhead resistance holds tight. Now the last two candles have been making newer lows, and we have closed a candle beneath the 8 EMA once more—a bearish signal. Though we have broken out of the channel to the upside, insufficient information exists for us to take a long stock position. *Patience to wait for the right signals will be invaluable every time.* It saves us from the train wreck.

The outcome of the situation can be seen in Figure 13.4. When the stock fails its breakout and returns to the original channel that it came from, it will confirm that the break to the downside continues. The moral of the story: price is an important element to consider,

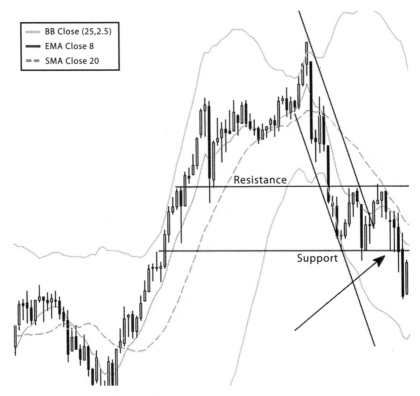

Figure 13.4 **Downside Break Continues**

and though we have confirmation everywhere, if price does not follow through for us, the trade setup is weak.

Let's consider another similar formation in Figure 13.5. The
chart displays the same type of downtrending channel, lower highs
and lower lows, and then a halt to the lower lows and sideways
action. I have defined a tight area of support and resistance by the
parallel lines labeled. Again, with all our channels, we are looking
for the signal to go long above or short below the downtrending
channel. The sideways channel action does not tell us which way
things might break. We are in a standing hold with no evidence of
any consequence in either direction.

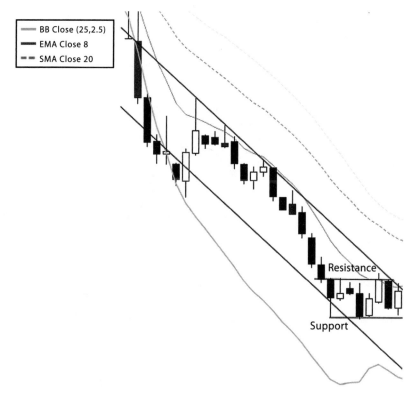

Figure 13.5 **Standing Hold**

Two candles ahead, and we have some evidence to usher in a decision in Figure 13.6.

What evidence do we have to go long in Figure 13.6?

- Two confirming candles above the 8 EMA
- Two candles above relative resistance
- Strong candle movement: four white candles showing higher highs and higher lows

What might be in the way of a long, or what might cause the long trade to fail?

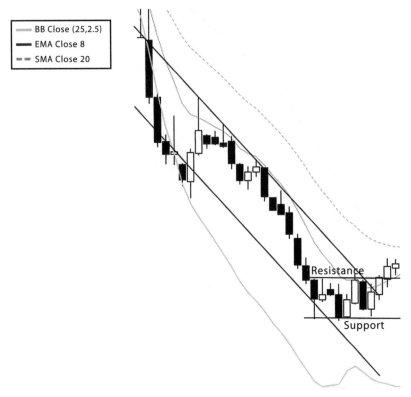

Figure 13.6 **Strong Candle Movement**

- 20 SMA above resistance
- Long trade would be countertrend

Here's a question: if this stock breaks out, where is the most likely place it will move to test? Mark it on the chart in Figure 13.6. If we ask ourselves this question, it may stop us from entering the trade. Ask: *why* am I taking this, and *where* is it going? The solid trade would be to enter half size, and at the confirmation candle print above the 20 SMA, go to full size. The conservative trade would wait for the break and confirmation candles to print above the 20 SMA.

Let's look at Figure 13.7 and see if we were right to take the long position.

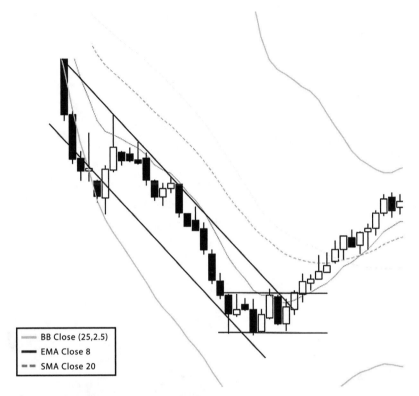

Figure 13.7 **Long Position in Parallel Formation**

Yes, according to the chart, we were. If there is one kind of trade that will give us the greatest bang for the buck, it would be these types of parallel formations. If we read them correctly, they will deliver, but it is important that nuances and particulars are observed.

HIGH-PROBABILITY CHART FORMATIONS

Once we become familiar with the technicals we use, the challenge for us is to not lose sight of all the signals that we need to keep track of in order to make accurate trading decisions with our trading system. Here, we'll take a look at some special formations that are particularly successful. Most of them will be familiar, but how we set the stage for movement may add another powerful weapon to our trading arsenal.

The Channel and the Flag

By far, the channel formation is a favorite of mine—it is easily identified and can be traded in a variety of ways. Consider the chart in Figure 13.8.

Look at the top right where I've drawn two channel formations. I am most confident in the break signaling a move above the wider channel, but the tighter channel shows real candlestick congestion.

Figure 13.8 **Channel Formation**

Channel trading rules look like this:

- **The third candle should point to the likelihood, so keeping careful eyes on the charts is always advised.**
- **The first candle close above the channel triggers the breakout.** If we are comfortable with assuming a larger stop, we can take the long trade here, but our exposure to risk widens because our stop is just outside the bottom of the channel, the area of relative support.
- **To trade this formation most successfully, we should seek out an entry that is at a bounce off the support range to go long.** Knowing that we might encounter resistance at the top of the channel, our most reasonable move, should we decide to go long, is to enter half size, then full size at the breakout and retest. We'll use the inverse of this logic to take the short trade at the rejection of the top of the channel in half size, and increase to full size at the breakout. As a side note, these three candles might make us think that the stock will break to the upside as the series makes higher highs and higher lows, but our top black candle is quite negative, retracing more than 61.8% of the white candle. Let's say we're tentative, and we are willing to accept the higher stop, waiting for the break of the wider channel levels.
- **Once the break occurs, and the candle closes, we are able to enter half size as we anticipate a retest of the level broke.** At the confirmation candle, we can add to the trade. Notice, I am not adding our other technical indicators we follow because I want to focus on the raw formations. Our strength of trade will do nothing but increase when we use the skills we are learning outside of these observations.

In Figure 13.9, the candle breakdown shown at the arrows confirms the break and closes well below nearby relative support, where we can enter half size.

Notice in Figure 13.10 how the trade continues. Channel breakdowns or breakouts are highly reliable; they may retest the levels but often continue in the direction of the break.

The more volume associated with a channel break, the higher the likelihood of short-term continuation in the direction of the break. Sometimes, the continuation moves forward without returning to test, but more than not, the stock will come back to test the breakout level. At other times, it recaptures the level and moves out and through the original channel, like the one shown in Figure 13.11, on page 220.

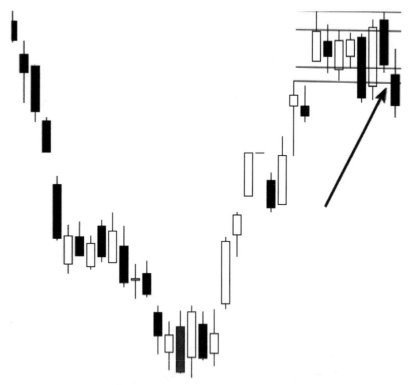

Figure 13.9 **Candle Breakdown**

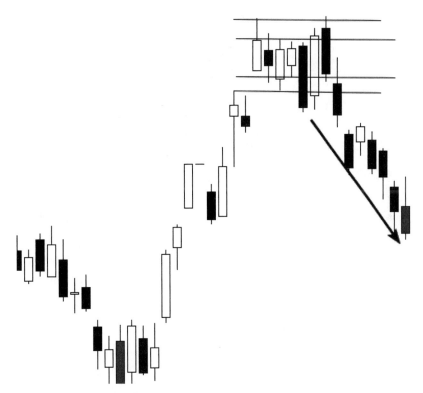

Figure 13.10 **Trade Continues**

If the channel has slope, it is called a flag, but the rules are exactly the same—we are keen on the break outside the established range of the trade. Note the formations and the breakouts in Figure 13.11.

The Volatility Squeeze

Channels can also be seen as a short series of dojis. Channels formed by these special candles create the potential for powerful breakout events. When the channel formed has small dense candlesticks with tighter ranges than the stock is used to seeing, this is called a *volatility squeeze*. (See Figure 13.12.) When a stock breaks out of this special

Figure 13.11 **Flags**

Figure 13.12 **Volatility Squeeze**

channel, it runs with a high degree of reliability, and it is rare that it comes back to test the breakout levels in the short term.

The Breakaway Gap

The next extremely powerful formation is the breakaway gap on volume, as seen in Figure 13.13. Breakaway gaps can occur to the upside and the downside. The rules are remarkably simple here, as this kind of movement usually is evidence of fundamental weakness:

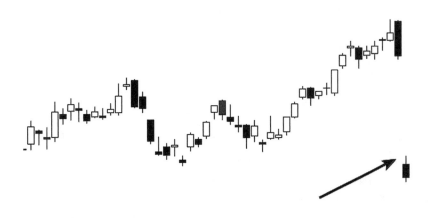

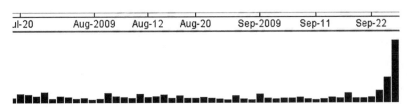

Figure 13.13 **Breakaway Gaps**

- If we notice large volume on the break, we watch the following day to see if it is able to recapture the high of the breakaway candle, and if it rejects, we are able to enter half size.
- If the chart fails the low of the initial breakaway candle, we can add full size and use our Fib levels to walk down to future targets.
- As long as the trade does not break relative resistance above, or below (if the trade is long), suppport, we can ride the trade down through the Fib levels.
- Breakaway trades may test resistance or support, but it is rare that they breach to recover at the initial outset. The stops can be set tight, and the momentum is relatively steep.

CONCLUSION

We've stepped through a number of trades in this book so far. Notice the form used to move through the trades: clear, quantifiable steps. A systematic approach is the foundation of consistent, successful trading. When we learn to order our thought structure through the trading process, we establish control over our side of the elements—and control will destroy our fears of trading. As we press forward and continue designing and orchestrating our trades, let's force ourselves into the habit of systematic thought—it will reap excellent rewards.

A Recap of the Technical and Temperamental Skill Sets

> "I know quite certainly that I myself have no special talent.
> Curiosity, obsession, and dogged endurance, combined
> with self-criticism, have brought me to my ideas."
>
> —ALBERT EINSTEIN

We've considered a number of technical indicators, so let's review them quickly to keep essential points in mind.

BOLLINGER BANDS

Volatility is always an important consideration as it will also define your stops. The volatility squeeze is an excellent high-probability trade, so be alert to diminishing width of the bands. Acceleration is slowing in the direction of the trend if the stock begins to print new highs or new lows that are away from the band. This will send

the mental alert to watch for the shift in trend. Swift expansion in the bands is a sign of significant price change that may or may not continue. If the price change occurs after a tightening of the bands, that is, a funnel-shaped Bollinger band, the stronger the likelihood of continuation. When the price pierces the Bollinger band at either the top or bottom, it *will* reverse. The strength of the reversal is associated with the power of the current move afoot and the wave rhythm the stock is tracing.

CANDLESTICKS: KEY ELEMENTS

Keep a grasp of the fact that candlesticks portray the emotions in the charts at a deeper level than the entire chart. Keep alert for long wicks at the end of breakdowns or breakouts. Though candle close and open are critical in analysis, failure to observe wicks will allow relevant support and resistance to slip by on occasion. Work to identify formations as quickly as possible—key formations we have discussed are the channel and volume expansion. The more swiftly we identify these, the greater the probability of success.

COMBINATION SIGNALS

Short, tight doji candles at the top or bottom of a trend on high volume usually signal a reversal on the way. A series of inside and outside candles side by side on constant volume and long-tailed dojis also signify breakout or reversal on the horizon. Higher volume appearing with Bollinger band expansion is an alert to continuation and potential strength of move.

DETAILS, DETAILS, DETAILS

The largest technical problem we will encounter in our trading careers will be our lack of attention to details, our lack of precision and timing. As we know, it's the details that destroy the money-making

opportunities for us. Though tedious, our ability to go down the list of questions at the end of Chapter 12 and answer them as quickly as possible will enhance the chances that our trade will go well.

FIBONACCI ESSENTIALS

Fibonaccis do not define the trades—they set the parameters. Poorly drawn Fibs are useless, though they may work in a hit-and-miss manner. The longer the time frame used to draw the Fib, the more important the levels, and trading according to these longer levels means a swing trade by default. Establish the wave in progress. Fit your Fibs to levels of support and resistance in the chart. Fibs are not always best low to high but often can reveal very important price events using congestion-to-congestion levels. Fibs may not initiate the trade all the time, but the Fibs will always identify the most advantageous price to enter *provided* the setup is holding. Fibs regularly signal the beginning of exits, as well as additions and subtractions from the position.

FROM THE BIRD'S EYE TO THE MICROSCOPE

By no means exhaustive, but certainly sufficient to enter into a position prepared, some additional questions to ask are: Is the market moving in the same direction as the stock trend? Is the stock confirming direction through several time frames? Have key areas of support and resistance been identified? Have volume patterns been considered? Does the stock have any impending news, earnings, calls, or dividends? Has the proposed trade been identified as trend or countertrend? What are the slopes of the 8 and 20 exponential moving averages showing? Is there a full cycle of Fibs from the weekly charts forward to the time frame considered for trading? Have the Fibs been fitted? What are the prior day's high and low? Are there any other congestion areas? Has stock volatility been assessed to determine the need for wider stops?

"IN THE TRADE" CHECKLIST

To avoid the "Crud, I wish I would have gotten out of that trade when I had the chance" and the "Crud, why did I leave that trade so soon" events, consider the following: How certain is this trade, or how many rules did the trade follow, or break? Go through the checklist of the system rules in Chapter 12. After we understand the market and can really trade, we can violate a few of these, but try not to violate any as a newer or growing trader. FYI, even the best of us should consider ourselves as growing traders. No violation means more confidence, and less questioning. More confidence means stronger decisions. Stronger decisions mean better trades and greater returns. Don't leave the trade before it is broken. Watching every single candle? Probably should stop doing that. Moving back and forward between time frames and changing parameters of the trade when nothing requires that? That's micromanaging. Passed the targeted exit and feeling greedy? Don't let that circumvent the need to trim the position; paper wins can turn to real losses in the moment a stock rejects a level. Conscious of any fear or anxiety affecting the ability for clear thought?

If we were foggy on the answers here, it means review of prior chapters is necessary. Perhaps a less passive approach to the material is required. We don't learn trading being passive, but we seem to approach instructional material very passively.

MOVING AVERAGES: KEY ELEMENTS

Moving averages define momentum. The golden rule remains "no slope, no trade." I give great assurance here that far fewer trades will fail if this is held as the cornerstone of decisions. Keep alert for acceleration, and the steepening curve seen moving averages drifting apart, and slowing, moving averages getting closer together, which leads to the well-known moving-average crossover. The first, acceleration, will tell us that our trade direction is strengthening, while the latter, closing distance between moving

averages, will alert us to momentum shift in the stock. Use a moving average that provides a level of comfort. If trading too much is a concern, perhaps instead of the 8 and 20, use the 15 and 30, and be aware of inflection events. My system is all about precision, but dialing back the need for action, if desired, is also an option. Let the candles confirm by closing two of them above the moving average or closing two below the moving average. The first candle will represent the breakout or breakdown, and the second candle completion will be the signal to move. Remember this, if the candles are above the moving average and the position is long, the trade will be green, and gains will accumulate. If the candles are below the moving average and the position is short, the trade will be green, and gains will accumulate. A key point to keep in mind is that if you are long in a trade and your candles are printing below the moving average, or if you are short in a trade and your candles are printing above the moving average, the trades are most likely on the wrong side and losses will accumulate. Most important, parabolic movement—moving average almost straight up, or straight down—*will* reverse, and moving-average inflection will send the signal for that. It is suggested that the choice of shorter moving average (8/20) crossovers is better; longer moving-average (50/200) crossovers are for systems less swift and will strip profit from the positions.

MULTIPLE TIME FRAMES

Mixing up the time frames on which we trade is extremely hazardous to our positions delivering profit. To keep things clear, use the longer time frames to determine overall trend, thereby identifying where the wind will be at our backs, and the short time frames to define our entries and exits with precision. Keep several time frames in view as stocks will reverse against these averages across tighter time frames, or we might follow the red-herring candle that will shake us out of the trade. Nothing quite makes for a bad mood like that.

PREPARATION: MENTAL AND PERSONAL

Lack of mental preparation, as we have discussed, is one of the primary reasons we fail. We are feeble trading machines if we are unable to set aside anger, either from being in a losing trade or when another person has gotten under our skin. Try to get adequate sleep and some physical exercise. Stay hydrated—it keeps our brains alert. Work at balance in life every day and make sure to take time to love the things that can love back. We spend too much time caring about things and people who cannot or will not reciprocate. What's a big account worth if we are lonely and empty inside? The balance between the things that really matter and the trading desk is a difficult balance for us, especially those who love everything about the markets. It can become our extracurricular affair, and we must keep the lines drawn carefully. Keep life in perspective. Check that ego. Our account sizes do not make us better, or more. This business puffs a lot of us up, so just know that the market is waiting to pull the rug out from under us, ready to send us through a wood chipper. Some of us need a good dose of humble pie. I know I did, particularly in the beginning of my trading career.

More key points to keep in mind: trading fearfully means trading poorly. It is guttural and, hence, very faulty. Fear can be eradicated with mental practice and proper preparation. When we consider a trade, plan out for worst-case scenario, instead of just best-case scenario. This means more than just setting the stops. Trades will go awry, so the more we hone our ability to catch the ball in left field, the more likely we are able to circumvent disaster. Rehearse the train wreck, and it will be as if we are seeing forward in time, before the trouble, so we can act.

Seek out the well-timed, well-executed trade. The money will follow. Don't be rushed to trade. Be patient, for the hundredth time. No, seriously, be patient and remember that stocks will generally retrace to certain levels. Learn to wait there for them like our stalker. Don't go looking for the mother lode or be afraid of missing out—the outcome there is that we chase everything and end up with nothing. We want to follow, not lead. Before each execution of *every* trade, ask, why am I trading this, and how many of my rules are in place? *Every trade, every time.* The more rules we find that we are breaking, the more likely we are to be entering a failing trade.

We will make bad trades. Get comfortable with that. Work at physical and mental exercises that minimize the loss of both physical and emotional capital and get you out of the "frozen in the spotlight" space. A long list to be sure, but each and every point is necessary to keep a grip on to achieve consistent, quantifiable success.

PREPARATION: PHYSICAL (TECHNICAL)

Physical preparation means identification of tradable information, a strategy for using the information, and a plan to execute the strategy. That's all. Scan the news for items deemed market moving, or stock moving, and isolate a list that is manageable. Start with one or two and five stocks at most, until you are able to trade those well. If we cannot trade five stocks well, we cannot trade well on the news concerning twenty stocks. We must filter what we allow into our heads. We can do this by avoiding listening to the pundits and talking TV so much, so that they don't influence what we see in the charts. Let's not collect so much information that we suffer information overload. More is not always better. Verify the validity of the trade—the "why" and the "where." Look for the high-probability trade. Leave the long shots alone. A little a day makes your trading capital stay.

RISK ASSESSMENT

This one is simple; but we forget it all the time. The more technical indicators that agree with each other, the larger the position size we can take. If there are conflicts around, we must lighten our initial entry, and when the signals confirm, enter with greater size.

SETTING YOUR STOPS

If we don't master setting stops correctly, it does not matter how good the system is, success will be absent or nominal. Resist the urge to take a larger size and set a tighter stop. Tighter stops will lead to more losses. Let me say that again. Tighter stops will lead to more losses. Determine the stop region first, then back into your position with the appropriate number of shares. The rule of thumb here is—the longer the time frame of the trade, the wider the stop necessary. Set different stop levels for portions of the positions. When I stalk an entry, my initial stop is usually quite tight, and when I have assumed a full size, I will frequently set a very tight stop for a quarter of the position, a midrange stop determined by recent wave retracement in my time frame for one-half, and finally a longer wave retracement in my time frame for the last stop. Trading a position does not mean an "all or none" stance. This, I have noticed, is a very difficult concept many of us must continually work at grasping.

STOPS, SIZE AND RISK

Does the proposed stop make sense? Has a real walkthrough of worst-case scenario been completed? Are you comfortable with the maximum potential loss? If there is no comfort with the position size, it is too large. Go back to the stops and recalculate what is appropriate. Sure as the day is long, not completing this part is an accident waiting to happen.

VOLUME

Volume will always define the strength of the move. Contrary to general belief, however, it will not identify the failure of the move, especially if we are trading to levels as we do with our market positioning system. Lack of volume at the point of a breakout does imply a retest of the breakout level. As a trader or investor, we should always be conscious of volume, but it should not keep us from entering the trade.

We rarely enter full size in our setups, and if we expect the retest, we can simply wait for it. As I often say, a stock is going where it's going, and sometimes it will just meander along the way, pulling back and pressing forward. Many of us miss out on nice price movement due to the fact that we are overly concerned about volume. Volume exhaustion and volume confirmation—two totally different events that begin with the same trigger: high-volume candles—can be confirmed only by evaluation of the candles that come right after the appearance of the original high-volume candle. Be on high alert so that jumping on the wrong side of the trade does not happen. When the candle formations show breakout, volume will usually direct us on the likelihood of a retest of broken overhead resistance or broken support. It is often the case that the more volume observed, the less likely it will be to test the breakout region. This does not mean that it will not retest that level. Commonly, we see that when important levels are broken, they are very often retested to establish new real support or resistance. Be sure to observe whether volume is constant, declining, or inclining, as this alerts us to the continuation of strength.

heart means believing in the self, knowing that even if the skill isn't there, we have enough strength of will to develop the skill, to manage defeat, and turn it into success, somehow, somewhere, someway. Believe it or not, talent is the lowest requirement on the list. There are many more gifted traders who have gone by the wayside because they lacked heart.

The more we experience defeat, the more we expend our energy without positive results or measureable gain. We lose the drive to continue onward to the completion of our goals. This is true of any endeavor in our lives: we need positive feedback to keep moving. We exhaust our emotional capital in trading by experiencing losses coming from poor trades and poor risk management. It is a shame that the cause of this drive reduction comes from a lack of skill, knowledge, and temperance because we could build that beforehand if we only knew we needed it to win this game.

Trading is a game of charging forward and yet restraining ourselves, a delicate balance, a strike between prudence and valor. We come with a specific set of mental equipment when we begin this endeavor. That equipment can only hold so much of a "will to defy defeat" measure within us, and it weighs one gram less than the size of the sandbag that can knock us over. If we've been tried by fire in our lives prior to beginning a trading career, we have a good idea of what kind of setbacks will stop us, but we underestimate the power of the blows the market can wield.

As with all attributes, each of us holds more or less emotional capital, but whether or not we have an abundance of it does not matter. What we have, we must guard carefully, but how to do this as newer traders escapes us. The answer again boils down to the management of exposure to risk. So often I say this, but we want to get to the end so fast that we're always playing catch-up as we fall further behind.

EMOTIONAL CAPITAL AND ITS EFFECT ON PHYSICAL CAPITAL

We, as traders and people, are going to experience loss; this, we know, but how much we lose is in direct relation to the blow to our intangible capital. What this implies is that the key to managing emotional capital is how we take on risk. I meet a lot of people with the desire to trade well—some tell me they come with a burning desire—but many fall to a rout because that desire is not coupled with drive or discretion.

I worked with a gal once awhile back who had some talent at reading charts. She had a rough start but had some good gains and a series of wins. Her wins made her more bold, and as with many of us, careless. She chose a running stock at the open and jumped in on margin, counting on a big win to start the day but neglecting to watch for reasons that moves may fail. The market is a different animal every day, and there is nothing like a little success in the market to lead us to huge failure. Always keep in mind that there are a plethora of reasons that a trade may fail, and keep your eyes open to catching them. She did not, and as the stock move reversed, she had patience with the loser and gave it room to fall further until she could no longer take the pain and left the trade significantly in the red. I never saw her trade again. She had drained enough physical capital to completely deplete her emotional capital account. When we realize that these two accounts are tied together, and our risk management of our cash account has a direct impact on our emotional account, we'll begin to be smarter about our trades and will avoid being a casualty of war.

MANAGING OUR EMOTIONAL CAPITAL

Our failure to manage emotional capital will destroy our ability to last through the ups and downs. This is not simply knowing our stops and general risk; it's knowing that you can handle the loss if it slips by your stops. I watched a video of Paul Tudor Jones once during his trading days. I believe the footage was filmed on a day he lost 6% of all his holdings. His body language showed a bit of a broken will for the day, head leaning against hand, tearing his glasses from his face to leave them dangling from two of his fingers, but it was for just a moment, and then his head snapped back straight up. He took a long visible breath, and he began to look to the day ahead of him.

He was preparing for tomorrow. Perhaps he reevaluated himself for a long while behind the closed door of his bedroom that night. I'll never know, but after that moment of the realization of staggering loss, after the bell and the trading, in the face of defeat, he chose to step over the momentary obstacle and look to the next day.

We spend so much time looking at our setbacks that without becoming conscious of it, we live our trading life in the rearview mirror. Last time I checked, driving while looking in the rearview mirror always makes for nasty crashes. Trust me, this one I know! Look forward, pay attention to the road signs, and when times are rough, trades go bad, and thoughts get terribly negative, stop driving for a bit and remember that looking behind never makes for better driving ahead.

TAKE A BREAK

We suffer market addiction, most of us—it is terribly difficult to unplug from the alluring whirlwind. We are so concerned about missing some great move while we are away, and we know when we return that it takes days to get our rhythm back sometimes. Furthermore, when we are struggling traders, there is some sense of urgency to trade every day. We have to be in something.

I just mentioned to someone that I do not trade every day because some days the market is best left alone. The response? Well, what am I going to trade when you're not trading? Luckily, the conversation was via e-mail or he would have heard my laughter. *We do not have to trade every day.* If we somehow feel that if we are not trading then we are not working, then we are doing something wrong. The action of simply observing markets all day long is work in itself. Fact: some days, it is better to preserve capital by not trading than to jump into the uncertain fray. Get used to it.

Then there is the actual vacation from trading. Leaving the market completely alone is one of the *best* remedies for poor trading I know of. Seems counterintuitive, but it is true. Something happens to our minds when we stay in a state of frustration, confusion, and uncertainty. It makes our decision making weak, and we begin to be unable to see clearly the scape in front of our eyes. I liken it to being in the middle of an argument and not being able to see both sides unless you become an observer. I spoke to a very good but quite young trader once about vacations. He said he hated them because their aftereffects were always longer than the vacation itself. He would lose the market rhythm, and so much happened without him, so he didn't take them. Wouldn't you know a year later he was at his wits' end and finally took a vacation? I tried to tell him—but there are those things that we must come to know on our own.

We need respite from the market, no matter how much we think we do not. After 12 rounds, it's time to get out of the ring, to heal, to think, to plan, and to prepare our minds for the next bout. Without a break, we are like a boxer in a fight of undefined length. Whether our 12 rounds last 6 months or 6 weeks, as soon as we feel tired of trading, just worn out, and our consistency begins to falter, it is time to take a breath from the frenetic market activity. Get away from the demanding environment of live trading.

Taking a break does not mean still sitting in front of the desk and paper trading, or studying, or doing chart analysis—that is not taking a break. Take a real break so that the mind becomes clear. Extricate from the market tentacles *completely*. It will breathe new life into your decision-making abilities and resolve to sit through a trade giving you difficulty.

Answer this question honestly: when's the last time you took a break? Maybe you say you don't need one because you're doing just fine. I am here to assure you that no matter how well you are doing, taking a vacation will make everything just a little better—if not a lot.

SUPPORT STRUCTURES

Support is one of the most important things in the world of trading. Frequently, the mentally demanding and physically exhausting elements of this work leave us empty shells at the end of the day. The only way we can replenish our psyches, especially after a tough day, is in the comfort of those who can understand us or the work that we do. For the person who has not day-traded or worked actively in the market, I can unequivocally say that though you might appreciate the work or love the person who trades, you cannot know the real feelings of isolation and bewilderment when the market does not behave as planned. Only traders know how other traders feel, and it is the rare case that there is complete disclosure of struggles and losses daily between the trader and his or her mate.

This lack of understanding adds an entirely new level of pressure that does nothing to help us perform better. At times, it is so destructive that one step forward and three steps back is what we take, always playing the catch-up game. Though the exceptionally strong person can carry on alone, traders need support structures, no matter if it is other traders, coaches, or loved ones. But it must be someone.

Trading is a dreadfully lonely business, and before Twitter, it was a virtual vacuum if the trader was not already connected with a trading group or membership. But Twitter is both a blessing and a curse. It provides us much-needed interaction with others who have chosen to do what we do, but it bombards us with so much noise that it frequently interferes with any chance of good trading. When I suggest filtering the noise, I know that it will be a difficult feat as we cleave to that special interaction. We, traders, know things that the world has no clue of. The online trader environment sheds so much light on truth in the market that we find ourselves chuckling at conversations we overhear. But this knowledge isolates us from normal interaction with others outside the field. We live and breathe and eat the market, and sometimes it feels that when we are not at our desks, we are simply going through the motions of other events in our lives. For many months, before I learned balance, when I left my desk, it was all I thought about—now it's just *mostly* everything I think about.

The trader reading this knows exactly what I mean. We are a special breed unto ourselves, different from the "market enthusiast," or economist, or market analyst, or any of those periphery occupa-

tions that touch trading, dabble, or talk about it. They might talk, but we put our essence at stake every day. We open ourselves to psychic damage and liquidity damage every time we enter the fray. How we anchor support in our lives as we trade is incredibly important.

CONCLUSION

As traders, managing our emotional capital is vital to our success, and, in the end, our sanity. It's difficult for us to step back and take a breather, but sometimes that's exactly what we need to do. Just because we aren't actively trading one day does not mean we are not working. Moreover, taking an actual vacation from our trading life can have huge benefits, not only emotionally but also for when we return rested, clear minded, and ready to trade again. So take a break. You probably need one and don't even know it.

Just as important, we need to maintain a level of support in our lives, or we will find ourselves in an incredibly solitary pursuit. Make sure the support structures are strong, and if they are not, consider redirecting energy into something that can bolster the spirit instead of tearing it down. The moment that the tearing down begins, the doors to destruction open wide.

Conclusion

"Knowledge is of no value unless you put it into practice."
—ANTON CHEKHOV

L earning to trade well is a lifelong endeavor, and choosing to be a trader as an occupation surely is one of the most adventurous things to do on earth. The reason so many of us fail is not only because we lack knowledge of the specific skills of identification, technique, and execution but also due to the failure to act upon what we know, largely because of our desire to never be wrong. There is a great deal of emphasis put on the psychology of trading, and rightfully so as we need to understand ourselves, but at the end of the day, we need to put to work the methods we know are successful. A simple decision—each one, and one at a time—and that's all.

We should accept that we will be wrong and manage the risk in case of this likely event. Most of us trade like we live, a little recklessly. We may find ourselves a bit on the edge, taking too much risk, and the younger we are, the more we are inclined to take on. We overindulge with foods even though we know it could give us a slew of maladies. We smoke even though we know it causes cancer. We drink even though we know it irrevocably damages our liver, brain, kidneys, and aspects of our personal life. We drive and talk on the phone even though we know we could cause an accident. We take part in a herd of detrimental behaviors. We're so used to living like this that we don't realize we gamble with our lives every day, some of us much more than others, but we all do it. We disregard the need for safety and live much too comfortably with risk exposure.

The absence of risk management in our lives bleeds over into trading, but the trading world is a place very willing to exploit the lack of attention to risk management. It is not a place to gamble with the outside chance. When we trade, we should forever be aware of the consistent set of guidelines that run the market. You must study them and know them better than anything else, learning the trading systems so well that the answers to questions blurt out even before that conscious thought. We then polish ourselves up through self-awareness and act on the recommendations provided by our trading systems.

Simple things—moving averages, Bollinger bands, and the Fibonacci levels—make an extraordinarily powerful trading system. The application of straightforward rules and a continued desire to learn more about the market will create mastery in a space where mastery is an anomaly. Trust me on this one, as I have traveled the well-worn road of retail trading, the fears associated with trading disappear with the complete knowledge of a good trading system and the subsequent application of its precepts. We must hold conviction in ourselves to apply the rules and prepare so much that second-guessing is an afterthought.

I'll leave you with this. Darrell Green still stands today as one of the most celebrated cornerbacks in the history of the NFL. Drafted in 1983 by the Washington Redskins, pundits deemed him too small at 5′8″, 170 pounds, to play in the league. Instead, he played for 20 years, has two Super Bowl rings from the Washington Redskins' wins in 1988 and 1992, and now is in the Pro Football Hall of Fame. Against all odds, and against competitors much larger, he rose to prominence. Green is characterized as a dedicated man who played every game like it was the last game he would ever play and from his early years was tireless in his preparation to be ready to get on the field. In an interview, he said something that I'd like to share:

"Prepare to be ready for your 'right now' moment," that moment when we are called to shine.

There is a line between mediocrity and distinction, and that line is called preparation—the wider and more pronounced the line, the further the distance between the two. If we trade every day, then every trading day will deliver us a "right now" moment, but for every moment that we choose not to prepare, choose not to learn powerful techniques, or choose not to develop the skills we already possess, we squander that moment away. Consider this book a call to action—to step from ordinary to extraordinary. All it will take is the decision to act on the knowledge you hold in your hand right now.

Glossary

15-minute rule: If a stock is exhibiting a trend, whether negative or positive, the 15-minute rule allows us to trade the breakout level above the high of the first 15 minutes or the breakdown below the low of the first 15 minutes. Prices tend to continue in this direction as long as slope exists.

Advance/decline: An indicator also known as *market breadth*, it measures NYSE advance issues and decline issues, revealing how many stocks are participating in a rally or decline.

Auction market theory: States that buyers and sellers will continue to move the market in one direction or another until the opposite force is motivated enough to step in and stop the advance. The market is in an auction. Price is set through a process called "price discovery." The market will auction as high as it needs to in order to find sellers or as low as it needs to in order to motivate buyers to see it as "relatively cheap." Description is defined by blogger FuturesTrader71.

Bear flag: Channels (see *channel*) that appear in downtrending charts; they have an uptrending slope. When a stock breaks out of the channel, it is a signal to enter a trade.

Bears: Traders who want the market to go down.

Bollinger bands: A "confidence interval" of most likely prices a stock is likely to print. It is plotted as a band of upper and lower bounds around a moving average. The closer a stock prints to the top or bottom of the band, the more likely a price reversal is on the horizon, creating a "bounce" off the bands (see *bounce*).

Bounce: A term referred to when in a downtrend, the stock price retraces some of the move, or bounces off a support.

Breakout/breakdown (aka b/o and b/d): Situation in which a price is trading within a consolidation pattern, hitting a resistance or support, and breaks through the area that was holding it within a parameter. *Breakout* usually refers to a break to the upside; *breakdown* refers to a break to the downside.

Bulls: Traders who want the market to go up.

Channel: A sideways price pattern that remains within levels of resistance and support. It can look like a rectangle (parallel) or uptrending and downtrending channels (parallel lines with slope), also called flags.

Chatter: When a stock prints prices in a close range; also called *range-bound prices*.

CL_F: Oil futures; will spike with severe weather conditions in the Caribbean or hurricane formations in the Atlantic or the Gulf.

Composite profiles: Profiles for volume (see *volume profile*) that can be mapped for individual days or by a collection of days that will combine all the prices printed and the associated volume and time frame with each price in the chart of any instrument.

Convergence: When two or more technical indicators confirm the direction of the trend, or confirm the impending change of direction, they are said to *converge* or *be in convergence*.

Daily pivot: A level in price calculated by the high, low, and close of the previous day. It gives a midpoint of the previous day's price action. Most charted pivots include related levels of support and resistance.

Day trade: A trade whose entry and exit are within the trading day.

Divergence: When two or more technical indicators conflict about the direction of the trend, they are said to *diverge* or *be in divergence*. Divergence often occurs before a trend changes, and technical traders watch for the reversal and the move to convergence, so they might trade on the break.

DVOL: NYSE decline volume, or volume of the stocks that are declining in NYSE.

DX_F: Dollar futures; are traded as other futures and often, though not always, have an inverse relationship to the slope of the broad market trend.

Elliott wave theory: Named after Ralph Nelson Elliott, it suggests that the market moves in a series of five waves and three waves. Fibonacci retracements (see *Fibonacci retracements*) measure these waves closely, and from the retracements, we are able to make decisions about entry and exit before the fact.

EUR/USD: The Euro and U.S. dollar pair; tells how many U.S. dollars are needed to purchase one Euro. As the dollar declines, the Euro gains strength. Dollar declines often, though not always, lead to increases in the market.

Fibonacci retracements: Patterns discovered in nature by Leonardo de Pisa that led to the development of Fibonacci numbers. Many traders commonly use these numbers to track the rhythm of the prices in the market.

Flags: See *channel*.

Gap: Created when a stock opens above the close of the prior day or below the close of the prior day.

Gap fill: When a stock moves through the price levels it has missed with the gap in price at the open.

Globex: Twenty-four hours of trading versus U.S. trading hours only.

Golden ratio: .618. From this level come all other levels in the Fibonacci retracement. The square root of .618 is .786, and the square of .618 is .382. The midpoint between .618 and .382 is .50. The square of .382 is .146, and so on.

High-volume node (aka HVN): A volume profile shows areas of high volume of trading in a price, as well as low volume. By definition, the volume point of control (VPOC), is the highest volume node. Any other areas of high volume are called *high-volume nodes*. High-volume nodes are significant because they will usually signify areas of "chatter." (See *chatter*.)

Initial balance (IB): A range that the futures will oscillate before beginning to trend. Much like the 15-minute rule, *initial balance* defines a range in the first periods of the day. An initial-balance area may occur in the first hour or the first 30 minutes.

Intraday trading hours: The time between the open of regular trading hours and closing of trading hours, 9:30 A.M. Eastern to 4 P.M. Eastern.

Long position: A purchase of stock, future, or option that implies the desire to see the instrument increase in value while holding. Long stock, short puts, and long calls are all long positions.

Low-volume node (LVN): A price at which there is low relative volume compared to other prices printing. LVNs represent areas of high-probability movement, with the rejection of the price if the stock/futures price is approaching the node from below, or a bounce from the price if the stock/futures price is approaching the node from above.

Market breadth: Advance/decline issues. See *advance/decline*.

Market positioning system (aka MPS): System taught in this book; a clear, concise trading system that identifies precise entries and exits.

Moving average: A technical indicator used to show the average value of price over a candlestick time frame.

Pennant: Also called a *triangle*, two converging trend lines that form an apex. The apex is the area that shows a breakout or breakdown and signals a trading event. When these lines do not converge before a breakout above or breakdown below, this formation is called a *wedge*.

Price action: Common term to describe price movement.

Print: A price that a stock is trading or has traded at; each price registered is called a *print*.

Pullback (PB): When a stock retraces prior levels in an uptrend.

Risk/reward ratio: A calculation to determine how much a trader is willing to risk for a predetermined reward target.

Scalp trade: A trade that you're in and out of for pennies.

Short position: A sale of stock, future, or option that implies the desire to see the instrument decrease in value while holding. Short stock, short calls, and long puts are all short positions.

Swing trade: Any timed trade that is not a day trade, from overnight to several months. A swing trade is not an investment.

Tick: A measurement of futures move. One /ES point equals to four ticks.

Tick indicator: The $TICK indicator is the difference between the number of stocks currently on the uptick and the number of stocks currently on the downtick. This tick is one trade.

Tick rules: These guidelines are simply signals. A tick extreme is a sign of strength/weakness (a reading of 1,000 or over or -1,000 or under). If there's a new tick high and price is not making a new high, this identifies possible divergence. This should not be the only identifier that signals a move. A tick high at a price high confirms the price high. When price is not making new highs and ticks are making new highs, it is a possible sign of strength. When the price is not making new lows and ticks are making new lows, it is a possible hidden sign of weakness.

Triangle: Also called a *pennant*, two converging trend lines that form an apex. The *apex* is the area that shows a breakout or breakdown and signals a trading event. When these lines do not converge before a breakout above or breakdown below, this formation is called a *wedge*.

TRIN: Short for Traders' Index. A technical analysis indicator calculated by taking the advances-to-declines spread and dividing that by the volume of advances to declines. If the value of this is less than one, then it is considered to be a very bullish indicator.

UVOL: NYSE advance volume, volume of the stocks that are advancing in NYSE.

Volume: An indicator used to measure the worth of a market move. The higher the volume during a price move, the more significant the move. It defines the number of shares or contracts traded during a given period of time.

Volume point of control: The highest point of volume that appears in a volume profile.

Volume profile: A technical stock indicator that shows the distribution of price in relation to the volume associated with the price.

Wedge: Also called a *triangle*, two converging trend lines that do not form an apex before the stock breaks above or below these converging lines. The break of these lines signals the trade.

Index

Note: Page numbers followed by *f* refer to figures.

Accountability, 64, 186–90
Actionable information, 7–8
Adaptability, 101
Advance, 245
Aggressive candles, 28
AlphaScanner, 143
Attention to detail, 101–2, 224–25
Auction market theory, 245
Aversion behavior therapy, 186, 191

Bear flag, 245
Bears, 245
Beta, 36, 139, 195
Bias, 3, 185
Black candles, 20, 21, 22f
Blindsight (film), 60–61
Blue Angels, 52
Bollinger bands, 35–39, 38f
    defined, 245–46
    for long trade, 115–21, 116f–121f
    and momentum, 36–37, 115, 116f, 117f,
        121, 166, 166f
    parameters for, 37–39
    range of, 35–37
    and reversals, 120, 164, 167, 224
    for short trade, 162–68, 163f–168f
    and stops, 116–21, 119f, 167f
    time frames and trends in, 197, 198
    in trading skill set, 223–24
Bounce, 246
Breach formation, 129, 129f
Breakaway gap, 221–22, 221f
Breakdowns, 218, 218f, 246
Breakouts, 39
    in channel trading, 217, 218
    defined, 246
    identifying, 209–11, 210f, 212f, 214,
        214f

and long trades, 127, 127f
and volume, 230–31
Breaks, taking, 236–37
Buffett, Warren, xiv
Bull flag, 119, 200, 208, 208f
Bulls, 246
Butler, Samuel, 59

Candlestick chart, 11f
Candlesticks, 19–28
    doji, 23–26, 24f, 25f, 224
    form and function, 20–22, 20f, 22f
    groups of, 26–28, 27f
    and moving averages, 160, 161, 227
    reading, 26
    support for, 22–23, 23f
    time frames of, 197–99, 197f–199f
    in trading skill set, 224
Capital, emotional and physical,
        233–39
Capital allocation, 68–69
Change, fear of, 99–100
Channels, 70, 71, 207–19, 216f, 218f,
        219f, 246
Chaos theory, 83
Chart formations, 207–22
    breakaway gap, 221–22
    channel and flag, 216–19
    identifying similar, 207–15
    volatility squeeze, 219–21
Charts. *See also specific types*
    and dissociation, 18–19
    noise in, 9
    strength of, 195
Chatter, 246
Chekhov, Anton, 241
Chin, Emperor, 98
CL_F (oil futures), 246

Collective unconscious, 26
Combination signals, 224
Competition, trading as, 30–31, 50
Composite profiles, 246
Confidence, 233–34
Confidence interval, 36, 245
Confirmation candle, 125, 126, 160, 168, 177
Congested support, 152, 153, 155f
Congestion regions, 86, 122, 169
Control, 205, 206
Convergence, 246
Coolidge, Calvin, 149
Corrective waves, 77, 80, 88f, 90, 152, 154f, 161

Daily pivot, 246
Daily time frame, 43f
Day trade, 246
Day traders
    expectations of, 54–56
    Fibonacci retracements for, 89
    mental preparation of, 49
    risk management by, 68–72
Decision making
    discipline and dedication in, 182–83
    discretionary, 48–49
    increasing competency in, 190–91
    responsibility for, 187–88
    and taking breaks, 237
Decline, 158–59, 158f, 245
Declining volume, 41, 42f
Detail, attention to, 101–2, 224–25
Discipline and dedication, 181–92
    and breaking your rules, 184–85
    in decision making, 182–83, 190–91
    and emotional exhaustion, 183–84
    and making mistakes, 185–86
    and mental preparation, 186–90
Discretionary decision making, 48–49
Dissociation, 18–19
Divergence, 246–47
Divine ratio. See Golden ratio
Division of funds, 65–67
Documenting your trades. See Trading journal
Doji candlesticks, 23–26, 24f, 25f, 224
DVOL (NYSE decline volume), 247
DX_F (dollar futures), 247

Econoday, 146
Edge, trading, 194–95
Einstein, Albert, 223
Elliott, Ralph Nelson, 247
Elliott wave theory, 76, 247
Emerson, Ralph Waldo, 207
Emotional capital, 233–39
    defined, 233–34
    managing, 235–36

and physical capital, 234–35
and support structures, 237–39
and taking breaks, 236–37
Emotional exhaustion, 183–84
Emotions
    and decision making, 188, 190–91
    in trading journal entries, 139, 141, 143
Endurance, 183
Entering trade checklist, 201–3
Entry points, 66–67, 72
    for channel trading, 217
    and Fibonacci retracements, 225
    for long trade, 109–10, 111f, 122, 124f
    for short trade, 154, 157
    and trading edge, 194
EUR/USD (Euro/U.S.dollar pair), 247
Exhaustion gap, 160, 161
Exit points, 72. See also Stops
    for short trades, 153–55, 168
    and trading edge, 194
Expectations, 6–7, 54–56, 183–84
Exponential moving averages, 32
Exposure
    to loss, 65–72
    risk, 202

Failure, 50–51, 96
Failure levels, 156f, 157, 170
Fast moving averages, 32, 34
Fear, 50–54, 99–100, 228
Fibonacci retracements
    accuracy of, 85–89, 87f, 88f
    defined, 247
    and inflection points, 77, 78, 80, 86f
    information from, 84f, 85f
    for long trade, 121–30, 123f–129f
    for short trade, 169–74, 169f, 171f–173f
    and stops, 122, 123, 126–27, 130, 170
    and support, 123, 124, 125f, 128, 129, 170
    in trading skill set, 225
    and waves, 82–91
15-minute rule, 200–201, 245
Fight-or-flight syndrome, 53
FinViz, 143
Flags, 219, 220f
    bear, 245
    bull, 119, 200, 208, 208f
Flanging, 116
Focus, 9
Following, leading versus, 100–101
Forgiveness, 97
Fractals, 78, 83
Franklin, Benjamin, 50, 190
Fundamental analysis, 3
Funds, division of, 65–67

Gambling, trading versus, 6
Gandhi, Mahatma, 47

Gap fill, 247
Gaps, 247
Gibbon, Edward, 75
Gilbert, Robert, 99
Globex, 247
Golden ratio, 83–84, 127, 176, 177, 247
Green, Darrell, 242–43
Green candles, 20

Heart, 233–34. *See also* Emotional capital
Heavenly ratio. *See* Golden ratio
Heraclitus, 1
High-beta stocks, 36, 139, 195
High-volume node (HVN), 247–48
Hood, Thomas, 193
Hourly time frame, 43*f*
HVN (high-volume node), 247–48

IB (initial balance), 248
Ideal trade setup, 193–206
    checklist for, 201–3
    daily routine preparation, 203–5
    and 15-minute rule, 200–201
    time frames and trends, 195–200
    trading edge, 194–95
Impulse waves, 77, 80, 87, 87*f*, 89–90
"In the trade" checklist, 226
Inclining volume, 41, 41*f*
Indecision, 52, 190
Inflection points, 77–78, 80, 85–86, 86*f*
Initial balance (IB), 248
Initial value condition, 32
Interpersonal skills, 97–98
Intraday trading hours, 248
Investors, 64–67, 89

Japanese candlesticks. *See* Candlesticks
Jones, Paul Tudor, 235–36
Journal, trading. *See* Trading journal

Keynesian economics, 4
Knee-jerk trading, 100
Korda, Michael, 135

Lagging indicators, 17
Leading, following versus, 100–101
Leonardo de Pisa, 247
Liquidity, 194
Load, 18
Logic, 4–5
Long position, 248
Long trade, 103–34
    Bollinger bands for, 115–21,
        116*f*–121*f*
    combining technical indicators for,
        130–33, 131*f*, 132*f*
    Fibonacci retracements for, 121–30,
        123*f*–129*f*

moving averages and general trends for,
    104–15, 104*f*–107*f*, 109*f*–111*f*,
    113–15*f*
as reversal of short trade, 149–50
Long-range candles, 23–24, 24*f*
Long-wick doji candles, 25*f*
Loss(es)
    and emotional capital, 234–35
    exposure to, 65–72
    and fear, 53–54
    journal entries on, 140–42
LVN (low-volume node), 248

Macro-view information, 12–13
Malkiel, Burton, 30
Manipulated markets, 11–12
Market breadth, 245, 248
Market maker, 40
Market positioning system (MPS)
    checklist for entering trades, 201–3
    defined, 248
    described, 16
    and mental preparation for trading, 49
    momentum in, 18
    and moving-average crossovers, 33–34
    and technical indicators, 15–16
Markets, 1–13
    changeability of, 1–2
    importance of learning, 17–18
    macro-view information on, 12–13
    manipulated, 11–12
    movements in, 75–82
    noise in, 8–10
    predictability of, 30
    reality versus perception of, 4–7
    surface of, 138
    and technical trading, 3–4
    time frames for, 10–11
    types of information on, 7–8
Mental preparation, 47–57
    discipline and dedication, 186–90
    and discretionary decision making,
        47–48
    and expectations, 54–56
    and fear, 50–54
    and success, 56
    and trading as competition, 50
    and trading as game, 48–49
    in trading skill set, 228–29
    and trading systems, 48–49
Mindset for success, 93–102
    adaptability, 101
    attention to detail, 101–2
    and beliefs about worthiness, 92–94
    fear of change, 99–100
    following versus leading, 100–101
    knee-jerk trading, 100
    negative self-talk, 95–96

procrastination, 101
stubbornness, 100
and treating yourself and others, 95–98
Mistakes
of new traders, 137–39
repetition of, 185–86
in trading journal, 140–42
Mob mentality, 26
Momentum
and Bollinger bands, 36–37, 115, 116*f*,
   117*f*, 121, 166, 166*f*
and Fibonacci retracements, 123, 124
and moving averages, 32–33, 114, 115,
   226
and trading edges, 194
and waves, 75, 90
Momentum trading, 16–19
Moving averages, 31–35
and candlesticks, 160, 161, 227
defined, 31–32, 248
for long trade, 104–15, 107*f*, 109*f*–111*f*,
   113*f*–115*f*
and momentum, 32–33, 114, 115, 226
and prices, 34–35
and pullback, 106, 106*f*, 108, 112
and reversals, 108, 114
for short trade, 153–62, 156*f*, 158*f*, 159*f*,
   161*f*, 162*f*
slope of, 32–33, 201
and stops, 108, 109*f*, 112, 114, 157, 159,
   159*f*, 160
and support, 110–13, 110*f*, 115*f*
in trading skill set, 226–27
types of, 31–32, 34
Moving-average crossovers
defined, 33–34, 226, 227
and long trades, 107, 114
and short trades, 154, 155, 161, 162*f*
MPS. *See* Market positioning system

Negative self-talk, 95–96
Noise, in markets, 8–10
NYSE advance volume (UVOL), 249
NYSE decline volume (DVOL), 247

Oil futures (CL_F), 246
Opinions, xiv, 8–9
Order, in markets, 4

Paper trading, 73
Parabolic exhaustion, 199
Parabolic expansion, 113, 113*f*, 199
Parallel formations, 215, 215*f*
Parameters, for Bollinger bands, 37–39
Patience, 188–90, 228–29
Patterns, in technical trading, 3–4
PB. *See* Pullback
Peaking events, 121

Peale, Norman Vincent, 233
Pennant, 248, 249
Perception of markets, 4–7
Personal preparation, 228–29
Physical capital, 234–35
Physical preparation, 229
Plutarch, 29
Preparation
daily routine, 203–5
and fear, 51–54
importance of, 242–43
mental. (*see* Mental preparation)
and patience, 189–90
personal, 228–29
physical, 229
Price action, 248
Price discovery, 245
Price rejection, 210
Prices
and Bollinger bands, 36
and moving averages, 34–35
range-bound, 246
and volume, 39
Pricing, value, 40
Primary waves, 77
Print, 248
Printed (term), 20
Probability bias, 3
Procrastination, 101
Pullback (PB)
and Bollinger bands, 167
defined, 248
and Fibonacci retracements, 127, 129
and moving averages, 106, 106*f*, 108, 112
Pullback waves, 77, 80

Range, in trading journals, 143
Range-bound prices, 246
Red candles, 20
Rejection, 163, 210
Relative stops, 69, 70, 108, 109*f*
Relative support, 70, 167*f*
Resistance
and breakouts, 211, 211*f*
for long trade, 123, 124, 125*f*
for short trade, 166–68, 170
and support levels, 69*f*, 70–72
Retail traders
expectations of, 183–84
mindset of, xiii–xv
Retest patterns, 231
Returns, expectations of, 6–7
Reversal candles, 21–22
Reversals
and Bollinger bands, 120, 164, 167, 224
and Fibonacci retracements, 174
and 15-minute rule, 200–201
and moving averages, 108, 114

Risk assessment, 229
Risk exposure, total acceptable, 202
Risk level, 64–72
Risk management, 59–73
    by day and short-term swing traders,
        68–72
    division of funds and exposure to loss,
        65–67
    establishing level of risk, 64–72
    importance of, 241–42
    and responsibility for decision making,
        187
    and rules, 60–64
Risk/reward ratio, 249
Rogers, Will, 15
Rules
    breaking your, 184–85
    and risk management, 60–64
    tick, 249

Scaling, 112, 113, 114*f*
Scalp trade, 249
Schwab, Charles, 93
Shaken out of a trade, 37
Shannon, Brian, xiv, 143
Short position, 249
Short trade, 149–79
    Bollinger bands for, 162–68, 163*f*–168*f*
    combining technical indicators for,
        175–78, 175*f*
    Fibonacci retracements for, 169–74,
        169*f*, 171*f*–173*f*
    moving averages and general trends for,
        150–62, 151*f*–156*f*, 158*f*, 159*f*,
        161*f*, 162*f*
    as reversal of long trade, 149–50
Shorting stocks, 40
Short-term swing traders, 67–72
Simple moving averages, 31–32
Slope, 18, 32–33, 37, 201
Slow moving averages, 32
Smith, Adam, 4
Social support, 237–39
Standing hold, 213*f*
Stocks
    high-beta, 36, 139, 195
    qualifying, 201
    researching, 138–39, 143–45
Stops, 66, 230
    and Bollinger bands, 116–21, 119*f*,
        167*f*
    in day trading, 69–72
    and Fibonacci retracements, 122, 123,
        126–27, 130, 170
    and moving averages, 108, 109*f*, 112,
        114, 157, 159, 159*f*, 160
    relative, 69, 70, 100, 109*f*
    trailing, 71–72

Strength
    of charts, 195
    shift of, 25–26, 25*f*
Stubbornness, 100
Subwaves, 79*f*, 81*f*
Success, 56. *See also* Mindset for success
Supply and demand, 21, 40–41
Support
    and Bollinger bands, 166, 167*f*
    and candlesticks, 22–23, 23*f*
    congested, 152, 153, 155*f*
    and Fibonacci retracements, 123, 124,
        125*f*, 128, 129, 170
    and moving averages, 110–13, 110*f*, 115*f*
    relative, 70, 167*f*
    and resistance levels, 69*f*, 70–72
    and trends, 152, 153, 155*f*
Support structures, traders', 237–39
Swing trade, 49, 249
Swing traders, short-term, 67–72

Technical indicators, 15–45. *See also* Chart
        formations
    Bollinger bands, 35–39
    candlesticks, 19–28
    for long trade. (*see* Long trade)
    and market positioning system, 15–16
    for momentum trading, 16–19
    moving averages, 31–35
    for short trade (*see* Short trade)
    time frames for, 42–44, 196–200
    in trading skill set (*see* Trading skill set)
    and trends, 29–31
    and volume, 39–42
Technical trading, 3–4, 16–17
Tenberken, Sabriye, 60–61
Thresholds, 65
Tick, 249
Tick indicator, 249
Tick rules, 249
Tight-range candles, 24*f*
Time frames
    for ideal trade setup, 195–200
    for markets, 10–11
    for technical indicators, 42–44, 43*f*,
        196–200
    in trading skill set, 227
    and trends, 44, 195–200
Total acceptable risk exposure, 202
Traders. *See also* Day traders
    journals of new, 137–39
    retail, xiii–xv, 183–84
    short-term swing, 67–72
Traders' Index (TRIN), 249
Trading
    knee-jerk, 100
    momentum, 16–19
    technical, 3–4, 16–17

Trading blind, 63–64
Trading checklist, 201–3
Trading edge, 194–95
Trading journal, 56, 135–47
  and improving decision-making, 190–91
  journaling process, 142–46
  of new traders, 137–39
  recording mistakes in, 140–42
  reviewing trades with, 135–36
  sample entry, 145–46
Trading skill set, 223–31
  attention to detail, 224–25
  Bollinger bands, 223–24
  candlesticks, 224
  combination signals, 224
  Fibonacci retracements, 225
  "in the trade" checklist, 226
  mental and personal preparation, 228–29
  moving averages, 226–27
  multiple perspectives on trade, 225
  physical preparation, 229
  of retail traders, 183–84
  risk assessment, 229
  stops, 230
  time frames, 227
  volume, 230–31
Trading systems, 242
  evaluating, with journal entries, 144–45
  failure of, 50
  and mental preparation, 48–49
Trailing stops, 71–72
Treating yourself and others, 95–98
Trends
  on candlestick charts, 26–28, 27f
  for ideal trade setup, 195–200
  for long trade, 104–6, 104f–106f
  for short trade, 150–53, 151f–155f
  stable and unstable, 66f, 67f
  and technical indicators, 29–31
  and time frames, 44, 195–96
  and waves, 76–82
Triangle, 248–50

Trigger points, 122, 170, 171f
TRIN (Traders' Index), 249
Tunnel vision, 26, 184–85
Twain, Mark, 1, 103
Twitter, 238

Uncertainty, 51
UVOL (NYSE advance volume), 249

Vacations, 236–37
Value pricing, 40
Visualization, 52–53
Volatility, 24, 106, 106f, 223
Volatility bands, 36. *See also* Bollinger bands
Volatility squeeze, 38–39, 176, 219–21, 220f
Volume
  declining, 41, 42f
  defined, 250
  inclining, 41, 41f
  NYSE advance volume, 249
  NYSE decline volume, 247
  and technical indicators, 39–42
  and trading edges, 194–95
  in trading skill set, 230–31
Volume point of control (VPOC), 247–48, 250
Volume profile, 250

Waisting, 116
Waves, 75–91
  corrective, 77, 80, 88f, 90, 152, 154f, 161
  and Fibonacci retracements, 82–91
  identifying, 76–82, 77f–81f
  impulse, 77, 80, 87, 87f, 89–90
  and market movements, 75–82
  and trends, 82
Wedge, 248–50
Weihenmayer, Erik, 60–61
White candles, 20, 21, 22f
Wicks, 224

Ziglar, Zig, 181